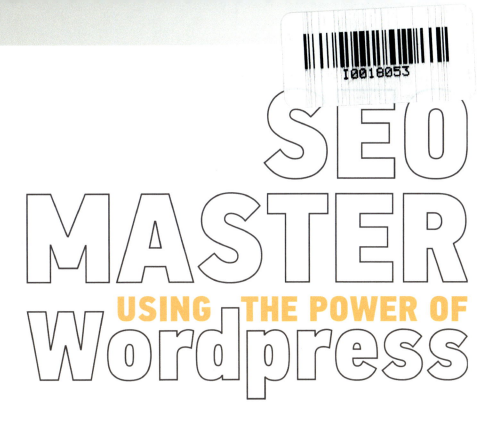

SEO MASTER
USING THE POWER OF
Wordpress

Konstantinos Kreouzis

Author of SEO Master Using The Power Of WordPress

SEO Master Using The Power Of WordPress
Copyright © 2012 by Konstantinos Kreouzis

ISBN-13: 978-960-93-3770-0

Author: Konstantinos Kreouzis
Publisher: Konstantinos Kreouzis
Lead Editor: Eleftheria Galari
Photography: Dimitris Vlaikos
Layout Designer: Dimitris Makaratzis

The Book is available to readers at http://www.seomasterwordpress.com

Contents

About the Author

Konstantinos Kreouzis has a bachelor of computer science and has worked in IT for the last fifteen years. In 2000 he established his own company that mainly deals with web design and consulting services for business promotion through the Internet. Through his business experience and years of personal research, he has acquired specialized knowledge on how exactly the Google search engine operates pertaining to search results and user search queries. His knowledge in this field has helped his clients sell products and services much more quickly and easily, since their websites held better positions in the Google search results page than their competitors'. In 2012 and after twelve years of professional success and experience in SEO (Search Engine Optimization), he decided to write a guidebook on how anyone can create an SEO-friendly website quickly, easily, and free of charge through the use of WordPress CMS (Content Management System). He also explains in his book how to operate and promote your website so that it holds the best possible position in the Google search results page.

Acknowledgments

This book could not have been written without the support of my colleagues and friends. First and foremost, eternal thanks to Dimitris Vlaikos, my company's photographer, who helped me with the illustrations of this book and the motivation to publish it. Our long talks persuaded me into writing and publishing it, even though during that period I was going through the worst time of my life, after the loss of my mom. Also, this book could not have been published without Eleftheria Galari, who reviewed every single word, put them all together, and made some really great suggestions. Last but not least, I would like to thank Dimitris Makaratzis, the creative director of my company, for an incredibly cool cover and interior design. I would like to thank this outstanding team of good friends, responsible for making this project possible. I love you all.

What This Book Is About

This is a guidebook on how to create a **Google-friendly** website quickly, easily, and free of charge using the **WordPress** content management system. It will reveal to you all those simple things that Google loves. It will not show you magic tricks but it will teach you how to use content management techniques that, when followed word by word, will make Google love you. And when Google adores a website, it rewards it with a good position in the search results page during any user search query.

The aim of this book is to show and explain not only to the layman but also to the advanced user, in simple terms without the necessity of special knowledge, how to create and manage a website **the SEO way**. Step-by-step, and through the use of examples and tried-and-true techniques of content management, you will be able to successfully create a website which will appear in the first pages of Google's search results page and in the best possible position. This book will show even the least experienced user how to create and maintain a Google-friendly website using techniques and plugins thus gaining an impressive presentation and higher ranking in the search engine, resulting in more traffic. And as we all know, more traffic on your website means more sales.

This book will also teach you how to use keywords and phrases, title tags, social networks, social bookmarks, and other promotion techniques. The thing that is really crucial for your website is to get fast and direct Google search results leading to more traffic. This book will show you exactly what to do in order to drive more traffic to your website with the use of SEO techniques. As we all know, the best way to get more traffic is to appear in the first pages of Google's search results. All the chapters of this book include analytical descriptions that have both illustrations and examples. If you follow step-by-step the suggestions in this book, the road to success will open before your eyes.

In just 3 to 4 weeks you will see your website appear in the first page of the Google search results page and you won't believe your eyes—and all this without paying one cent for web marketing!

The Reason Why You Should Use WordPress As an SEO Platform

WordPress is crawler-friendly and that's a fact. One of the basic rules of SEO is that Google is a crawler and, like all search engine crawlers, it cannot read the content inside JavaScript and Flash presentations. So you must always remember that Google cannot fill in search forms, it cannot read links and menus that are made with JavaScript or Flash, and it cannot read any content embedded in pictures or graphics. By choosing WordPress to create your website, you avoid all of the above issues because WordPress does not use any of the above technologies in order to display menus and contents. In this way, WordPress is considered crawler-friendly for the simple way that it displays content. The platform structure makes all texts, menus, and links accessible to the Google crawler.

The Power of WordPress

WordPress is not simply a platform used exclusively for the creation of blogs as the majority of its users believe, but it is the ideal platform for the creation of any type of website, business or personal. You don't need to be a geek to post content, images, or even videos easily to the website in no time and with no special knowledge of exotic languages such as CSS, PHP, HTML, or Java.

The real power of WordPress is not the fact that it is easy to use but that it is built according to SEO basic guidelines. The developers who created it used an innovative technique. They divided its structure into two major categories. The first category is about the graphic design (theme) of the web page and the second one involves the content of the website. This is exactly why Google loves WordPress, because it doesn't need to search through infinite code pages concerning the design of the page to find the content, but instead it glides through it and finds reference to the MySQL database where the content lies. So Google saves time, which is really important in SEO terms.

WordPress's superiority lies in the fact that Google loves new content, so when it finds out that a website is built with the use of WordPress, it automatically assumes that new content will be regularly posted and therefore classifies it in a high-interest category and crawls its content frequently. The more frequently the Google crawler visits your website, the higher the number of pages that are registered in the index that Google keeps on its servers. When Google is going through the process of a user's search query, it does not go through all the websites of the world, in real time. Instead, it is searching in its own servers, where the content of the websites had been saved at an earlier time, when Google's crawler passed through them. So the more frequently the crawler visits your website, the more pages it saves in the search engine index.

What You'll Need Before You Can Begin

To begin the construction of your very own SEO website from scratch, you will need the following:

1   **A Domain name**

2   **A Linux based web server**

3   **Wordpress installation package**

4   **The latest version of Firefox web browser installed**

Preparing the Ground
Domain Name

My suggestion as to purchasing a domain name is the registrar company **GoDaddy.com** *(Figure 0-1)*. For a name such as www.mycompany.com, you won't need to spend more than $15.00 per year. I have been using GoDaddy.com for the past few years and it has proved to be an economical and reliable solution. Apart from that, during checkout it will give you recommendations on extra services that are quite interesting. However, I would not recommend them at this point. Just press **"no thanks"** and complete checkout. It is very important that your domain name include 1 or 2 words that are directly related to the subject of your website. If your dream name is not available, try using synonyms or derivatives of words that characterize the service/product of your website. For example, add to your domain name the city in which you reside, if you are addressing the local community, such as "Local Pet Shop & Nursery at Essex County": *www.essexpetshop.com, www.catanddogessex.com,*

Note: The domain name you choose should include 1 to 2 keywords relevant to the subject of your website www.essexpets.com, or www.essexpetshopping.com. You will learn more about domain-choosing techniques in *Chapter 1.* After purchasing the domain name from GoDaddy.com, you will need to wait about 2 to 3 hours for it to be activated and ready for use. While waiting for the activation of your domain name, you can proceed to the next step, which is the purchase of a **Linux-based web hosting plan.**

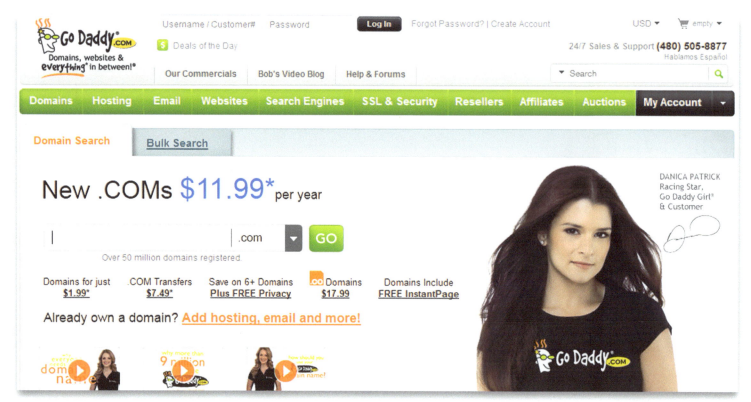

FIGURE 0-1

Linux-Based Hosting Plan

My suggestion on buying a Linux-based web hosting plan is the **Hostgator Company** *(Figure 0-2)* at http://www.hostgator.com. For a simple but service-satisfying Linux-based web server, you will not need to spend more than $20.00 per month for a package that includes unlimited domains, unlimited bandwidth, unlimited disk space, and more services. This service package provides you with a *"Shared web server plan",* which means that you will be sharing your server with other users. Alternatively, you can get a *"Dedicated web server",* which is a server that is exclusively yours at a cost of $200 per month. However, this is quite excessive for a new website. Most of my customers use shared plan servers and function large websites with 20,000 visitors per day with absolutely no problems.

Apart from its numerous services, Hostgator also has a simple control panel, known as **cPanel** *(Figure 0-3),* through which you can easily manage everything. On the cPanel you will also find a service called **Fantastico De Luxe,** which allows you to install the CMS WordPress platform—without downloading it to your computer and then uploading it to your web server using an FTP client and then setting it up. With the use of Fantastico De Luxe, installation and WordPress setup is done easily by using a wizard, with just a few clicks and with no special skills required.

FIGURE 0-2

FIGURE 0-3

Setting Up the Host for SEO
Connecting Domain Name With the Web Server

After buying the domain name and the web host, your next task is to connect the domain name with the web server. To do so, you need to declare the **DNS servers** of the hosting provider to the manager of the domain name, which in our case is GoDaddy. If you have bought a hosting plan from Hostgator, you must have already received an email with all the necessary information of your server (username, password, DNS server). Make a note of the two DNS servers (Nsxxx.hostgator.com, NSxxx.hostgator.com) and then go to GoDaddy's main page and log in. Then go to *"My Products"* -> *"Domains"* -> *"Domain Manager"* (Figure 0-4). Continue by clicking on your domain name *(Figure 0-5)* and process the name servers from the *"Name Servers"* button *(Figure 0-6)*. Lastly, choose *"I have a specific name server for my domain"* and type in the DNS server that was contained in the email you received from Hostgator and press *"OK"* to save the changes made *(Figure 0-7)*. 1 to 2 hours are needed for the new settings to be activated, but usually they are ready in less than an hour.

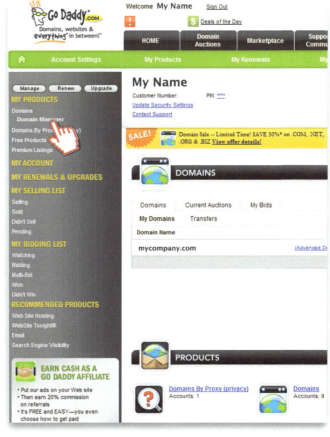

FIGURE 0-4

FIGURE 0-5

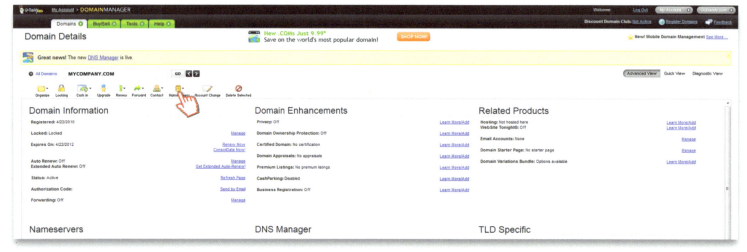

FIGURE 0-6

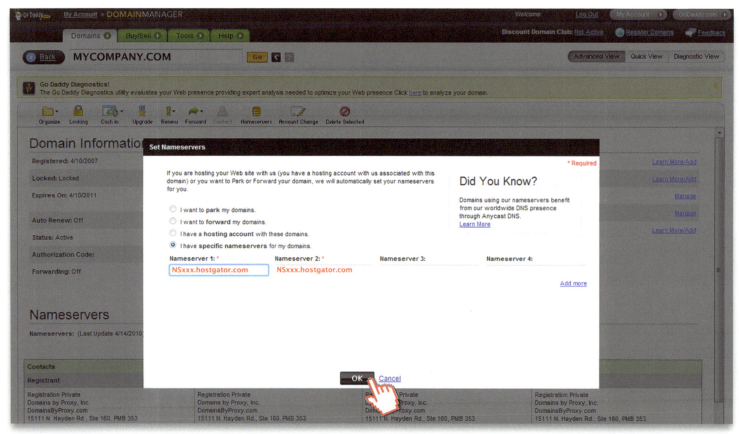

FIGURE 0-7

Installing WordPress
to the Web Server Using cPanel

If you choose Hostgator as your web hosting provider, or another provider that has **cPanel** as its management tool, then the installation process is done easily through **Fantastico De Luxe**. Fantastico will install WordPress and create your website's MySQL database and MySQL user automatically. You don't need to know how to create a database or how to create a new database user. Basically Fantastico will do all the hard work for you. Just log in to your web server management panel through your browser and then press the Fantastico button *(Figure 0-8)*. Then press on *"WordPress"* on the left of the screen *(Figure 0-9)* and go to *"New Installation" (Figure 0-10)*. Fill in all the necessary fields and press *"Install Word-Press" (Figure 0-11)*. Finally, press *"Finish Installation"* *(Figure 0-12)* and on the next screen fill in your email *(Figure 0-13)* to receive all crucial WordPress settings. Store or print out these settings for safety reasons, for example in case one day you want to transfer your website to a new host.

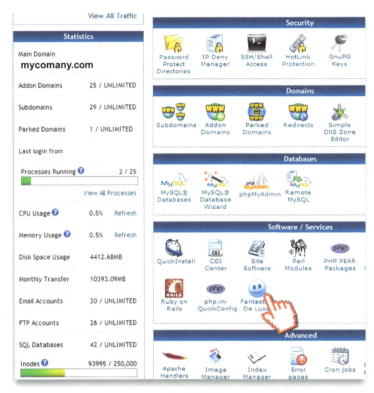

FIGURE 0-8

FIGURE 0-9

FIGURE 0-10

WordPress

WordPress

Install WordPress (1/3)

Installation location

Install on domain   **mycompany.com**   ▼

Install in directory

Leave empty to install in the root directory of the domain (access example: http://domain/).
Enter only the directory name to install in a directory (for **http://domain/name/** enter **name** only). This directory SHOULD NOT exist, it will be automatically created!

Admin access data

Administrator-username (you need this to enter the protected admin area)   **admin**

Password (you need this to enter the protected admin area)   **password**

Base configuration

Admin nickname   **your nickname**

Admin e-mail (your email address)   **your email**

Site name   **mycompany.com**

Description

Install WordPress

FIGURE 0-11

FIGURE 0-12

- Nucleus
- WordPress

Classifieds
- Noahs Classifieds

Content Management
- Drupal
- Geeklog
- Joomla 1.5
- Joomla
- Mambo
- PHP-Nuke
- phpWCMS
- phpWebSite
- Siteframe
- TYPO3
- Xoops
- Zikula

Customer Relationship
- Crafty Syntax Live Help
- Help Center Live

Please notice:

We only offer auto-installation and auto-configuration of **WordPress** but do not offer any kind of support.

You need a username and a password to enter the admin area. Your username is **admin.** Your password is **123456** The full URL to the admin area **(Bookmark this!)**: http://mycompany.com/wp-admin/

Back to WordPress overview

Email the details of this installation to:

your email

Send E-mail

FIGURE 0-13

Installing WordPress to the Web Server Manually

If you already have a hosting server without cPanel or Fantastico De Luxe, then you need to install the WordPress platform manually. Just download WordPress from http://www.wordpress.org *(Figure 0-14)*. Then go to http://codex.wordpress.org/Installing_WordPress *(Figure 0-15)* and follow the **Famous 5-Minute Install** tutorial.

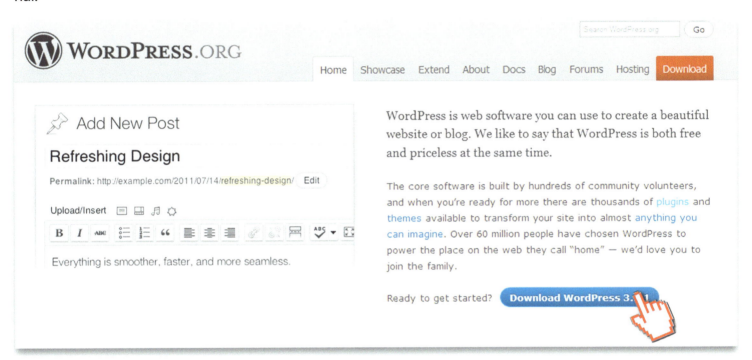

FIGURE 0-14

Famous 5-Minute Install

Here's the quick version of the instructions, for those that are already comfortable with performing such installations. More detailed instructions follow.

- 8.2 Software Appliance - Ready-to-Use
- 8.3 Easy 5 Minute WordPress Installation on Windows
  - 8.3.1 WAMP

If you are not comfortable with renaming files, Steps 3 and 4 are optional and you can skip them as the install program will create wp-config.php file.

1. Download and unzip the WordPress package, if you haven't already.
2. Create a database for WordPress on your web server, as well as a MySQL user who has all privileges for accessing and modifying it.
3. Rename the `wp-config-sample.php` file to `wp-config.php`.
4. Open `wp-config.php` in a text editor and fill in your database details as explained in Editing wp-config.php to generate and use your secret key password.
5. Upload the WordPress files in the desired location on your web server:
   - If you want to integrate WordPress into the root of your domain (e.g. `http://example.com/`), move or upload all contents of the unzipped WordPress directory (but excluding the directory itself) into the root directory of your web

FIGURE 0-15

Running WordPress for the First Time

After installing WordPress, go to your website's main page http://www.mycompany.com to check if everything is working properly. The default WordPress main page on your browser with the article *"Hello World"* *(Figure 0-16)* should be on your screen, and you are ready to move to the next step.

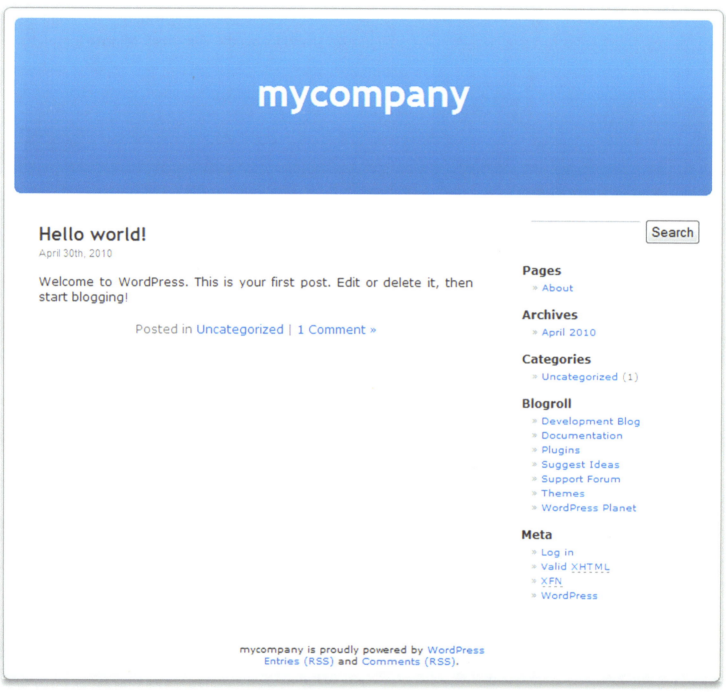

FIGURE 0-16

Accessing the WordPress Dashboard

Go to your website's control panel by typing *http://www.mycompany.com/wp-admin*. You will be asked to fill in the WordPress **username** and **password** *(Figure 0-17)*. After that your website's administrator page will open

FIGURE 0-17

(Figure 0-18). The WordPress **Dashboard** is a tool, that allows you to access easily all areas of your website. On the left side of the screen you can see the modules that can be expanded or contracted by clicking on the module title bar. These WordPress modules are responsible for adding or editing posts and pages, images and videos, managing your visitors' comments, changing the appearance of your website, adjusting the settings of WordPress installation and extending the capabilities of your website by adding plugins. When you expand one of these modules, more options will be at your disposal. In the following chapters, you will learn in details, with the use of examples, how to manage all these modules properly and, most of all, the SEO Way.

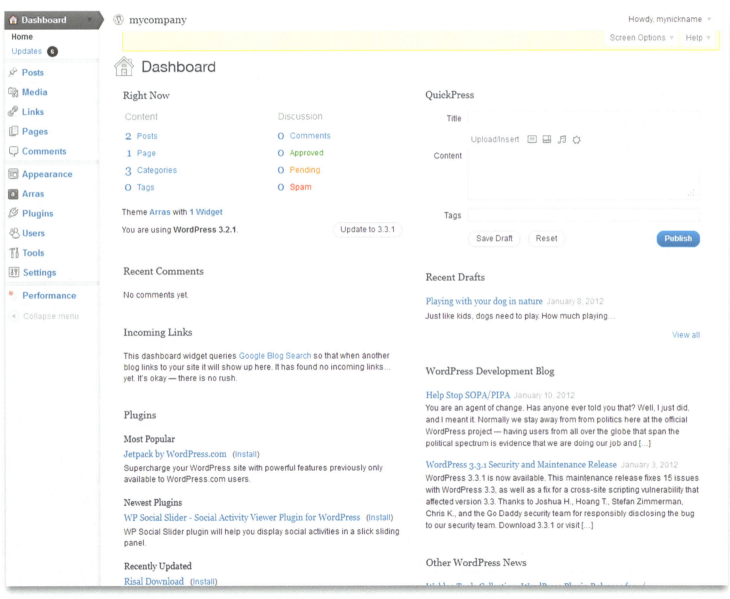

FIGURE 0-18

The SEO Philosophy

A Few Words About SEO

SEO (Search Engine Optimization) is the way to improve the organic traffic of your website, free of any marketing cost. This is achieved when your website appears among the first pages of Google's search results, during any search query, based on keywords.

Achieving the Goal of SEO

Achieving the goal of SEO is not something that can be achieved from one day to the next. It is a strategy based on web page management techniques as well as on the use of the suitable plugins, all working together. All of the SEO techniques are applied by the web page administrator and their effectiveness is directly related to the amount of time he or she dedicates on a daily basis. You can achieve the best possible position in Google just by applying rules based on years of research. In the following chapters of this book, I will explain to you in detail and with simple examples how to successfully make your website Search Engine Optimized (SEO) using the WordPress content management platform.

Patience Is a Virtue

To succeed in SEO, you must be patient, for many reasons. Here is one: according to researches, lots of static, old websites, long existing in Google's index, have an advantage against new websites, but only for a short period of time. That's because time matters for Google, and due to their long existence, Google considers these websites as very reliable. What is more, when these old websites embed working links of other websites, their reliability is boosted. Don't think you will climb onto the first pages of Google overnight. Time is a significant factor for Google, but you can overcome it, with patience and hard work. After a while, your SEO website will be discovered by Google, thanks to the use of the right techniques. These techniques are given in this book, leading you to success. So, as wine gets better through the years, aging is a very important process in SEO business, as well.

The King of SEO Is Keyword Research

Keyword research is one of the most important aspects of SEO. This is the case because people use keywords to search the Internet. Think about it. When you're typing a search query inside Google's search box, you are typing words, not sentences or phrases. That's why we must focus on good keyword research—because through keywords people search the Internet, and when they press the *"Google Search"* button, Google is also searching inside its huge database of websites, trying to find pages relevant to the keywords they have typed in.

Finding the Right Keywords

Adwords Tool - Word or Phrase Research

Keywords are the milestone of every good SEO strategy. Try to find the most relevant words to the subject of your website (five to ten at most), write them down on a sticky note, and stick the note on your monitor frame. Google provides you with a very useful tool at https://adwords.google.com/select/KeywordToolExternal *(Figure 1-1)* especially for keyword research. This tool shows you which words people search for more frequently, locally and globally. So use this tool and choose words relevant to your subject with high search frequency by Google users. Believe me, you don't want to use keywords on your website that people are only rarely searching for. Write a word or a phrase, for example type in *"pet shop,"* inside the first box and press Search.

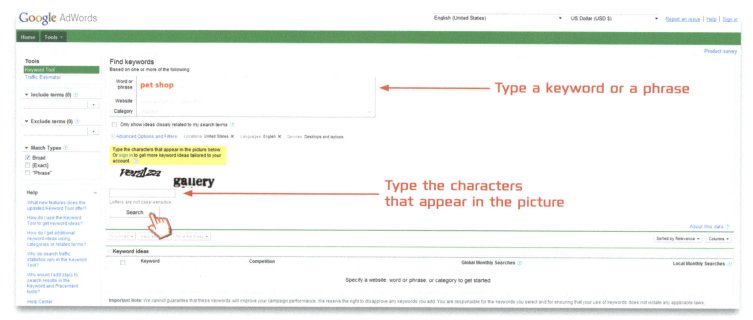

FIGURE 1-1

The search process came up with some numbers showing the global monthly searches of the example keyword phrase *"pet shop"* and some words relevant to it *(Figure 1-2)*.

Keyword	Competition	Global Monthly Searches	Local Monthly Searches	Approximate CPC
pet shop	Low	4,090,000	4,090,000	€0.25
net pet shop	Low	8,100	8,100	€0.36
pet shops online	Medium	60,500	60,500	€0.33
pet shop games	Medium	165,000	165,000	€0.18
jollys pet shop	Low	6,600	6,600	€0.42
jollies pet shop	Low	4,400	4,400	€0.47
the pet shop	Low	4,090,000	4,090,000	€0.24
pets shops	Low	201,000	201,000	€0.35
my pet shop	Low	40,500	40,500	€0.23

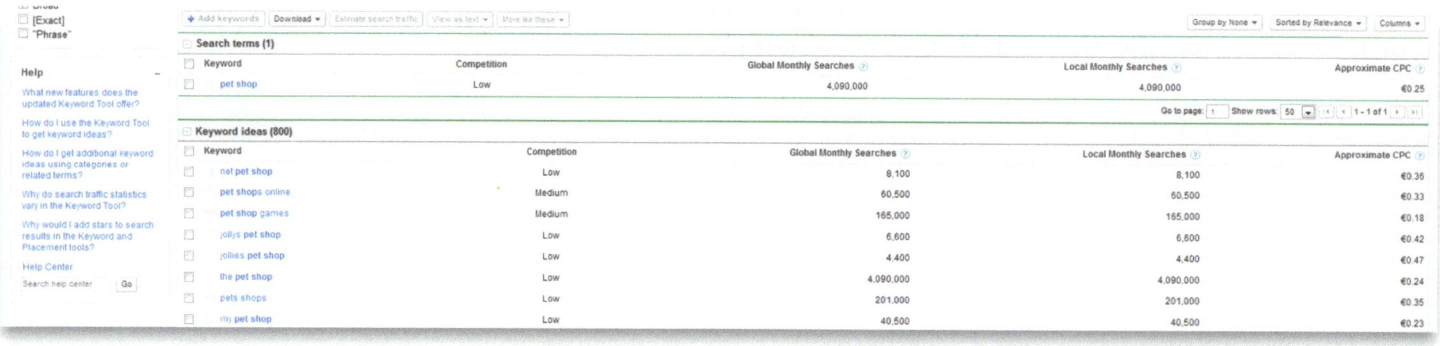

FIGURE 1-2

As you can see, the number of searches for the keyword phrase *"pet shop"* reaches up to 4,090,000 searches per month, which is quite significant. So, you can easily assume that *"pet shop"* is a very good keyword phrase, as many people use it while searching in Google, every month.

Now, check out the phrase *"littlest pet shop"* appearing in the search results list, with up to 823,000 searches per month. So the word "littlest" combined with "pet shop" gives us another popular keyword phrase.

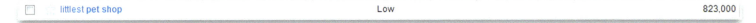

Use this tool and try out all the keywords you can think of, relevant to your website's subject. By studying the statistics, you can choose among the most popular ones and then use them as menus, titles, tags, etc.

Adwords Tool - Website Research

This same tool can also help you check your competitors' websites for keyword ideas. It works like a spy. By filling your competitors' URL in the box with the label *"Website"* and pressing *"Search,"* the tool will crawl this website for keywords and will list them for you *(Figure 1-3)* as it did with the word or phrase in the previous section.

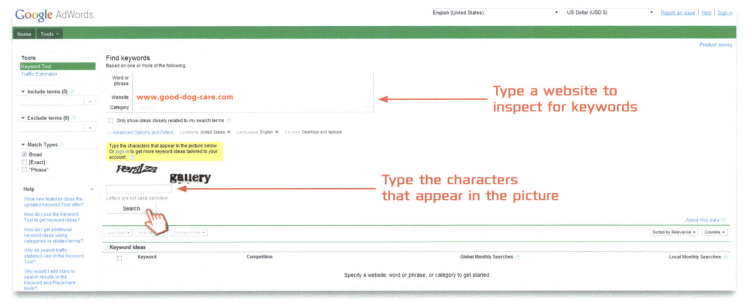

FIGURE 1-3

From that list you can find out what words your competitor is using and how important these keywords are for searchers *(Figure 1-4)*.

Keyword	Competition	Global Monthly Searches	Local Monthly Searches
potty dogs	High	22,200	18,100
training assistance dogs	High	9,900	8,100
training a rottweiler	Medium	6,600	2,900
assistance dogs training	High	9,900	8,100
stop a dog chewing	Medium	27,100	18,100
be a dog trainer	Medium	673,000	450,000
equipment dog	High	60,500	33,100
potty training dogs in 7 days	Medium	110	73
training a poodle	Medium	4,400	2,400

FIGURE 1-4

For many people SEO is a way of life, as they think and work the SEO way, and so must you. After a while, when you write an article or a headline, you will know right away which keywords are the best to use.

Operating WordPress the SEO Way

Tuning Up Your WordPress Website

So now that you have the keywords, it's time to begin with the basic Word-Press setup. Try to remember that everything we do from now on is based on SEO techniques. Log in to the administrator panel (dashboard) of your website at http://www.mycompany.com/wp-admin. Then navigate to *"Settings"* -> *"General"* and fill in all the fields.

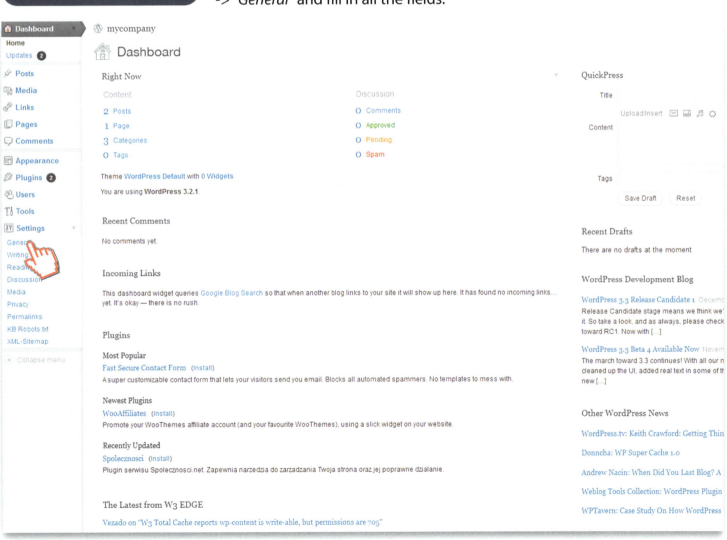

Site Title

Write a title relevant to the subject of your website. In this title you must use 2 to 4 of the main keywords you have chosen.

> Site Title

Tagline

Type the description of your website. At this point, you must use 6 to 8 of the main keywords you have chosen. This description will be the brief presentation of your website, the one that Google will display on the search results page when it hits your homepage. In Chapter 5, I will show you how to apply a specific description to each and every one of your subpages separately.

> Tagline

Wordpress Address (URL)

Just fill in *"www."* after http:// and before the domain name. It is an eye and typing thing. Users are familiar with URLs beginning with *"www."* because they see these kinds of URLs and type them all the time.

> WordPress address (URL)   http://www.mycompany.com

Site Address

Just fill in *"www."* after http:// and before the domain name. Again it is an eye and typing thing. Example: *http://www.mycompany.com*

> Site address (URL)   http://www.mycompany.com

Leave all other form fields as they are or modify them according to your needs and then press *"Save Changes."* After saving the changes, you will be asked again for the username and password. This is because you changed your website URL when you filled in *"www."* in the domain name field. Fill in your username and password again to reenter to the administrator control panel.

Privacy Settings

Privacy

Choose *"I would like my site to be visible to everyone, including search engines (like Google, Bing, Technorati) and archivers"* and press Save Changes *(Figure 2-1)*. By choosing this, you authorize Google and other search engines to access the content of your webpage.

> **Caution:** *Be extra careful and do not forget to select this option. Otherwise, your website will not be accessible by any search engine—WordPress will block all access rights to your website by adding restrictions to robots.txt.*

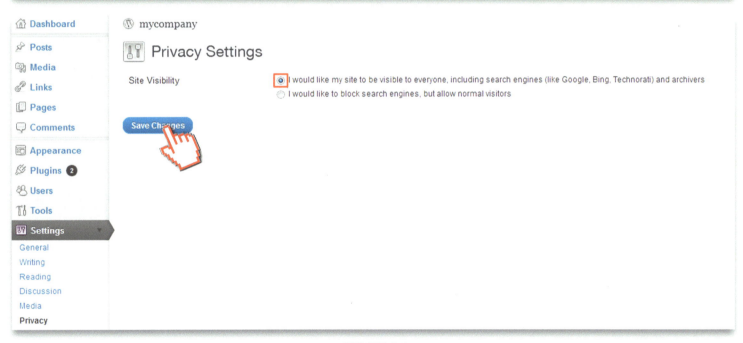

FIGURE 2-1

Permalinks Settings

Permalinks

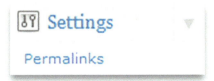

The correct use of permalinks is very important to the SEO process. During the search query, Google isn't looking for keywords only in the website's content, but also in its URL. So, by embedding keywords in your URL,

Google "sees" that you use the keywords in your URL that someone is searching for and automatically puts you higher up the results page list, up against your competitors. What is more, your URL will be user-friendly, as users will be able to read in it the keywords they are looking for, and therefore will automatically assume that the content of the page is what they are looking for. Read and compare the following URLs:

URL example with proper SEO permalinks settings

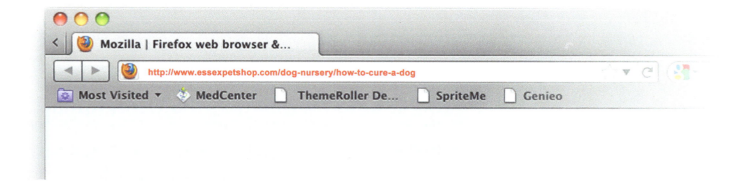

URL example without proper SEO permalinks settings

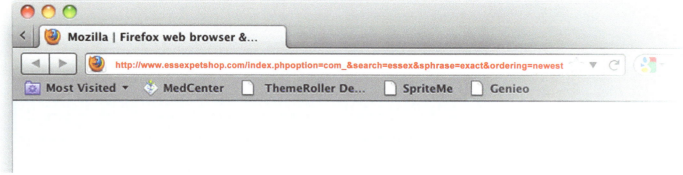

Which one is easier to read and write down?

To embed keywords in your URL, you need to change the settings in the permalink page. Select the field *"Custom Structure"* and type the following:

/%category%/%postname%/

By using this setting, the category name and the article title appear in the URL of each article. So the use of keywords in the category name and article title makes Google understand that you have what it is looking for, just by crawling your URL, and it ranks your website higher than your competitors'.

Creating & Managing Content

Categories

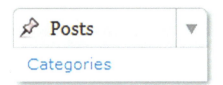

Categories are the backbone of your website upon which you will build your content. Due to the high importance of the categories, you need to apply SEO techniques, even here. To manage categories, choose *"Categories"* from the WordPress administrator panel *(Figure 2-2)*.

Note: Build the structure and navigation of your webpage based on keywords and phrases relevant to your website's general content

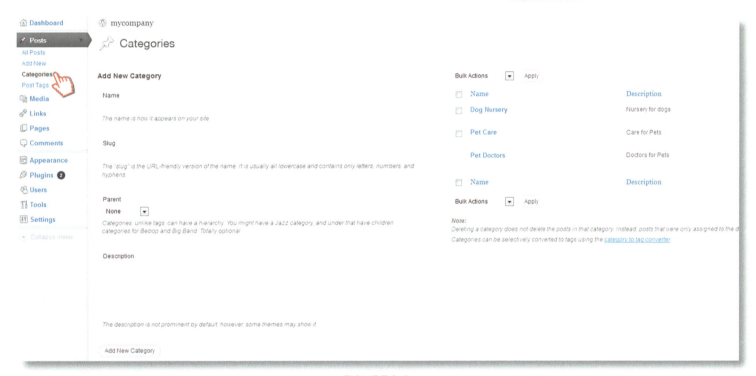

FIGURE 2-2

Category Name

Name the title of the category using the keywords you have chosen. The name of the category should not be longer than three words. Let's use our favorite example, the pet shop: *"Local Pet Shop & Nursery at Essex County."* The category name will not simply be *"Dogs"* but *"Essex Dogs," "Essex Dog Breeds"* or *"Dog Nursery."* Simply use keywords in each category name.

Category Slug

> Slug
>
> *The "slug" is the URL-friendly version of the name. It is usually all lowercase and contains only letters, numbers, and hyphens.*

This field modifies the appearance of the category URL. Specifically, here you can change the category URL into: http://www.mycompany.com/category-name/. Keywords must also be used here, because as already mentioned previously, Google sees and rewards them both inside the content of your website and in the URL. For example, a good Category Slug would be: *Dog-nursery*

As a result, your URL would look like this:

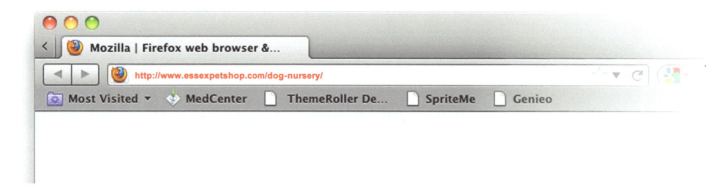

This way Google will get 5 keywords from your URL without even coming close to checking your webpage content (Essex, pet, shop, dog, nursery). I am sure you now understand how important the correct use of slugs is *(Figures 2-3, 2-4).*

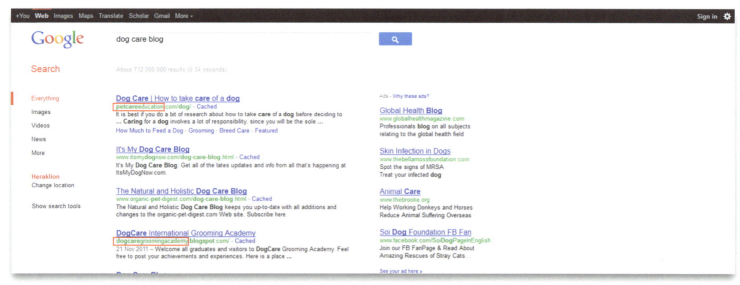

FIGURE 2-3

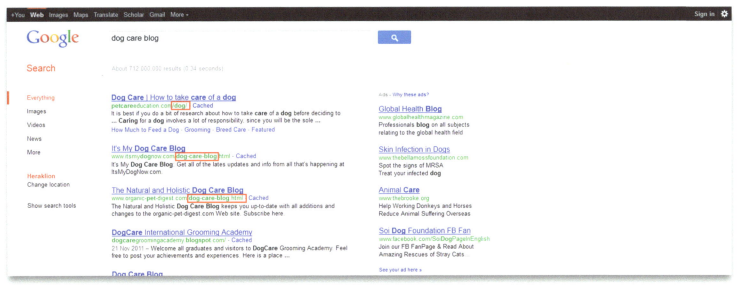

FIGURE 2-4

Category Parent

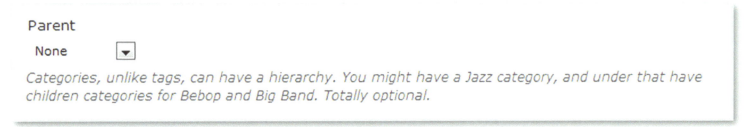

Every new category you are creating may be assigned to a Category Parent, in order to set up a hierarchy. Choose *"none"* if you are creating a main category; otherwise use the drop down list to choose the Parent Category to which the new sub-category belongs.

Category Description

Write down a short description of the category, including in it 2 to 4 keywords. Do not leave it blank. The description must be directly related to the subject of the category and should be at least 200 words. Create a good description that makes sense to the readers.

Posting Content the SEO Way

SEO 101 | Google Loves New Content

Create fresh, original, new content; always use different keywords relevant to your webpage content, and always target your readers. Initially, it would be great if you could write at least one original article every week—"original" meaning conceived by you and not copied from other websites. From then on, publish as much as you can, depending on the time you have. Continuous content publishing is for most people a very boring and painful task, but it is necessary to keep your website alive. The more content in your website, the more people will be interested in it. The more people are interested, the more Google focuses its attention to your website. Keep in mind that the keywords you use should differ from article to article because you run the risk of being considered a keyword spammer, something Google does not like at all.

In this chapter, I will explain in detail how to post new content to your website, based on SEO rules. Always remember: *Google loves new articles because it wants to provide its users with the best and latest content.* Make sure you publish new articles regularly, so that Google lists you under *"News Websites,"* which means that the search engine crawler robots constantly keep an eye on you. And believe me, it is very, very good for Google to have its eye set upon your website.

Posts Add New

Post Categories

All you need to do is choose the appropriate category for each article. If none of the available categories are suitable, you can easily create a new one, as explained in Chapter 2.

Post Title

When preparing your SEO strategy, it is very important to choose the appropriate post title. The title is one of the most important things for Google, if not the most important one. It is the text that appears in Google results, with bold, underlined blue letters *(Figure 3-1)*. That is why you must use as many keywords as you can in the article title. For example, if you Google *"dog care blog,"* among the first page's results will be a webpage with that exact phrase in its title. Note that the title that will appear in the search results page is not the one of the website's homepage, but it's the title of a specific article. From the example you can see how important it is to use keywords in the title of each article.

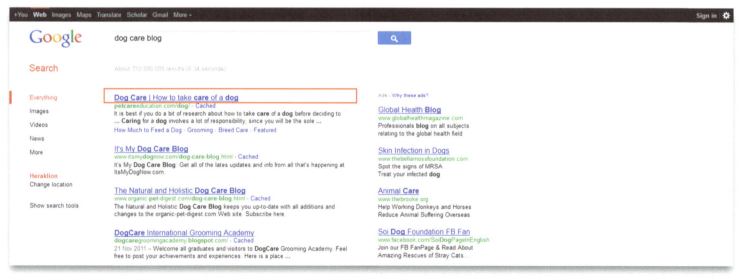

FIGURE 3-1

Adding Images | Upload/Insert

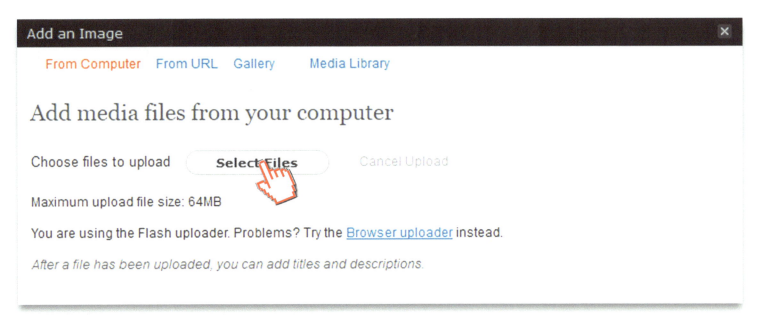

By using the ⟨Select Files⟩ button you can add images to your article. SEO techniques can be applied here as well, with the use of keywords in the file name and the image title. For example, instead of naming the image "IMG0001.jpg," it would be more effective to name the image *"dog-care-center.jpg."* Most users are looking for images for many reasons. So when a user is searching for a specific image, Google compares the words used in *"image file name"* and *"image title"* to the user's keywords. When the user clicks on the image, he is automatically transferred to your website. This way you get traffic not only from the web but also from the specialized image search engine. In chapters 5, I will explain in detail how to insert pictures into articles and how to use more advanced SEO techniques, like how to incorporate keywords into an image description.

Article Main Body

At this point, just write the article's text. In the text you must try to incorporate as many keywords relevant to the article as possible. There is no recipe for the exact number of keywords or for how often they should appear in the content's body. One thing is for sure, the keywords must appear in the content in a way that the article is grammatically correct and makes sense. If you use the same keywords too many times, Google will realize that you are trying to manipulate the search engine with meaningless text and will reduce the article's importance factor, which will lead you to a lower ranking in the Google search results page. Another setback of reckless keyword repetition is that your readers will see your webpage content as badly written and without meaning, thus they will not forward it to anyone, leaving unexploited another SEO technique called link popularity, which we will cover later on *(see page 27).*

Note: Publishing fresh and good-quality content is, was, and always will be the basic principle of SEO. Publish at least one post per week at first. The article content must be based on keywords and must target your readers and not the search engines.

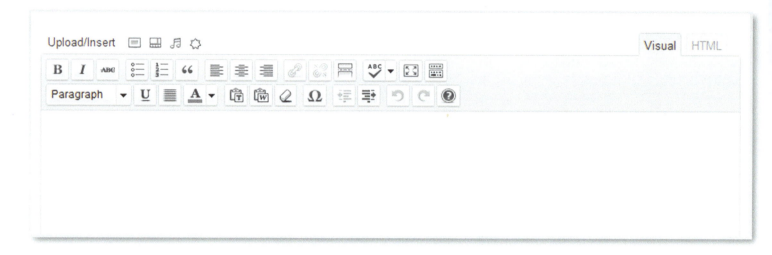

Post Excerpt

Most WordPress themes (the site's layout and design) are built in a way that, when a new article is posted by the editor, a part of it appears on the website's homepage, ending with *"Read more."* This helps the visitor take a quick look at a part of the latest articles on the homepage. If the command *"excerpt"* is embedded in your theme's code, then a summary of your article will appear on your homepage, with the indication *"Read more,"* which is automatically added by WordPress, linking this summary to the main body of the article. However if the command "excerpt" is not embedded in your theme in the first place, you must then fill it in yourself a brief summary of your article in the appropriate excerpt field, in the appropriate field, because you will need it in order to apply another SEO technique called *"Meta Description Tag,"* as explained in Chapter 5.

Post Tags

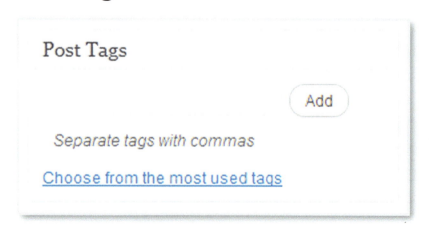

Note: it is commonly discussed lately, among most web promoters, that in the near future websites will be categorized by search engines, based on their tags.

Tags are yet another way to categorize your articles. So the visitor, instead of choosing a specific category, is now choosing a tag; and based on the tag, he or she is automatically linked to all relevant articles. Tags may appear either at the end of the article or on the right side of the homepage, in a place called the sidebar, as a widget. Using keywords is necessary, even here. In every article posted, you must always add 2 to 3 relevant tags. Tags may consist of 1 to 3 words, not necessarily forming a proper sentence.

Post Discussion

Discussion

☑ Allow comments.
☑ Allow trackbacks and pingbacks on this page.

The popularity of your article is another important factor, according to Google. By checking *"Allow comments,"* you allow your visitors to say how they feel about your article. This way, you can start a discussion, making the article larger and more important. Google "sees" the discussion unfolding inside the article, and automatically places it among the *"high interest"* ones, leading to a better ranking in its search result page.

Note: Google rewards websites that have links leading to other websites.

In addition to that, by checking *"Allow trackbacks and pingbacks on this page,"* you allow other websites or blogs to refer to your own article or to include the entire article in their websites. At first, this may sound bad, as it seems as though they are actually stealing your article, but in fact they are helping you climb up the ranking stairs, by applying in your favor another SEO rule called *"Link Popularity."*

The more the references to your website by others, the more important Google thinks you are. This is based on everyday communication; for example, if you ask a friend where to dine tonight, he will propose a nice restaurant, based on his past experience. He will not recommend one to you that has not satisfied him. In the same way, when Google finds lots of references or links to a website, it considers it to be important, like in the case of the nice restaurant. Finally, every time someone makes a reference or a direct link to one of your articles, a message appears on your administrator panel (dashboard), informing you of who is making that reference and asking you whether or not you allow him to do so. This is also the case when someone posts a comment.

Making Your SEO Website Cool

Changing the Theme

Since the basic settings of the website have been made and you now fully understand how to publish an article the SEO way, it is the right time to work on the template/theme of your website. In regard to the appearance, there is no SEO technique that can be used, for the simple reason that search engines do not care about how a website looks but rather are interested in what it contains. However, I will show you how to change the appearance of your website and how to apply several adjustments, in a way that its content is better displayed to both users and Google.

Appearance

Start by selecting *"Themes"* from the appearance menu on the Dashboard. Then press the Install Themes tab *(Figure 4-1)*. Choose among the different options, the specific features that better suit your taste, in regard to color, columns, width, features, subject, etc. and then press the Find Themes button.

FIGURE 4-1

In case you have not made up your mind on how your website should look, just press the (Search) button, without having chosen any of the above fields. Many different theme layouts will then appear. Choose one of them, by pressing the *"Install"* link under the theme's name *(Figure 4-2)*.

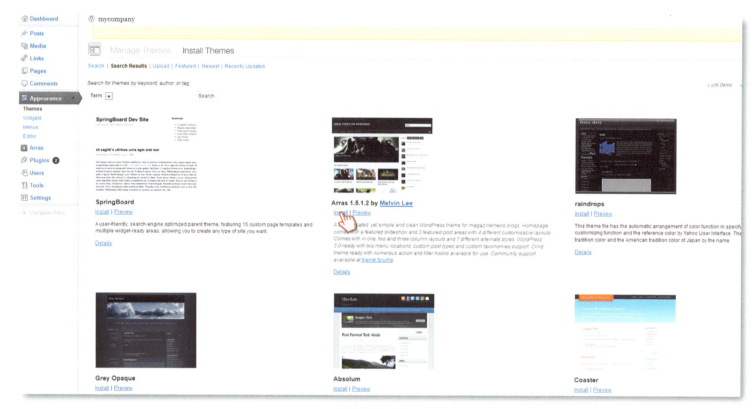

FIGURE 4-2

Then press the (Install Now) button, in the pop-up window *(Figure 4-3)*. On the next screen press the *"Activate"* link *(Figure 4-4) to activate the theme*. Now your theme is up and running and ready to be customized *(Figure 4-5)*. Check the tabs to see all available options for the theme and modify them according to your taste. The modifications you will make in the Options page of the theme are just a matter of your personal taste. If the theme you have chosen has a built-in options page, it will automatically take you to the theme's options page so that you can make the necessary adjustments to meet your needs *(Figure 4-6)*.

FIGURE 4-3

FIGURE 4-4

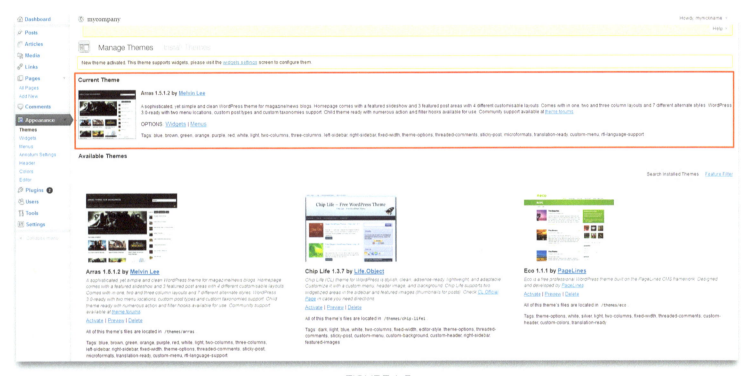

FIGURE 4-5

FIGURE 4-6

Advanced Content SEO Techniques

Global SEO-Friendly Meta Description

The specific part of the text that appears on the search results page, below the underlined link written in blue letters, is called the **meta description tag**. Obviously, this set of words is very important—not only because it is used by the Google crawler as a keyword resource relevant to the object of your website, but also because your potential visitors can take a quick look at what the article is about. In fact, this piece of description of your content, that appears on the Google results page, is actually the real estate *"property"* you own, which talks about you and is exclusively yours. Therefore, you must use a meta description tag in a way that gives your potential visitors a brief description of your website. Your meta description tag should be so catchy that no one can resist clicking his or her way into your website *(Figure 5-1)*.

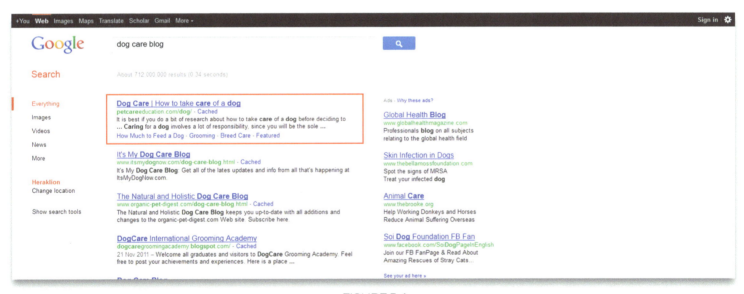

FIGURE 5-1

WordPress is using as a meta description tag, the description you previously typed in the field *"Tagline"* at WordPress's *"Options Page" (see page 16)*. The only problem is that this particular meta description tag refers only to the homepage of your website. But what about all the other pages of your website and the articles in them? What would be their Description Tag? The Google crawler collects from your website's pages and articles, what you have declared as meta description tag in code (PHP or HTML), for each one of them. When Google does not find a meta description tag, it either uses the one from the homepage, as WordPress applies by default, or makes one up using parts of the text included in the article. However, here lies a problem: the general description of your website is not suitable to all of your pages. Nor would it be right to let the crawler use random information collected from your content as a description tag. What is more, manually adding a unique piece of PHP code to each page as a meta description tag would be quite difficult and painful, even to the advanced user.

You can easily solve this problem by adding a piece of PHP code in WordPress. By doing so, you get the following results:

 When the Google crawler accesses your homepage, it will display on SERP (Search Engine Results Page) the default tagline that you typed in at General Options of WordPress.

 In all the other pages of your website accessed by Google, the crawler will be forced to use on SERP (Search Engine Results Page) the theme's excerpt or the summary that you have typed in yourself in the excerpt field (*see page 26*).

By using the following code *(Figure 5-2)*, you give your potential visitors an accurate description of each page's content, and you avoid projecting the same default description for every page, which would not be correct.

However, keep in mind the following:

 Make sure that the most important keywords are included early on each page, preferably within the first two sentences. This will ensure that those valuable keywords will be picked up by the search engines and hopefully pulled for whatever key phrases you are targeting.

 Make sure that the content in your post/page is in conjunction with your post/page title and does not contradict it. This will help solidify your post's/page's reputation with the search engines.

Meta Description Code

```
<meta name="description" content="<?php if (have_posts() && is_single()OR is_
page()):while(have_posts()):the_post();
$out_excerpt = str_replace(array("\r\n", "\r", "\n"), "", get_the_excerpt());
echo apply_filters('the_excerpt_rss', $out_excerpt);
endwhile;
elseif(is_category() OR is_tag()):
if(is_category()):
echo "Posts related to Category:
".ucfirst(single_cat_title("", FALSE));
elseif(is_tag()):
echo "Posts related to Tag:
".ucfirst(single_tag_title("", FALSE));
endif;
else: ?><?php bloginfo('description') ?>
<?php endif; ?>" />
```

FIGURE 5-2

Applying the Meta Description Code

The code must be added in the header.php file of your current theme in a specific line. One way to do that is by downloading header.php, then editing it and uploading it to the web server. However, you can do it an easier way, by editing the header.php file from the WordPress's appearance menu. WordPress provides you with an embedded editor so as to enable you to edit any file from within WordPress installation.

Consider that your current theme is Arras (as you have already downloaded and activated it, in Chapter 4). The next step is to insert the code in the Arras theme header.php file. From now on, if you decide to change the look of your website by activating a new theme, you must always repeat the following process.

From the WordPress Dashboard, go to *"Appearance" -> "Editor"* and then select the header.php file located on the right side of the screen *(Figure 5-3)*.

FIGURE 5-3

Then copy the Meta Description Code located in *Figure 5-2* and paste it on the line that reads **<?php arras_ document_description() ?>** in order to replace it. Press Update File to finalize the modification.

FIGURE 5-4

If your theme header.php file does not include the above-mentioned line in the exact same words, search between <head> and </head> *(see Figure 5-3)* for a line of code that contains the word *"description,"* and replace all of that line with the given code *(Figure 5-4)*.

In the next section, you will learn how to make the content of your articles even more attractive and Google friendly.

Adding Style & Links to Content

Extensive research has shown that Google pays great attention to style—to emphasized words embedded in the content and to the keywords that directly link you internally to a particular article.

So you as well must emphasize, in various ways, on some of the keywords you have inserted in your article. The styles you should use are bold, italic, underline, H1 headings, H2 headings, and H3 headings.

The bold, italic, and underline styles should be used accordingly in the first three keywords of your article.

The H1 heading, H2 heading, and H3 heading styles should be used in the titles contained in your article.

> **Caution:** do not use bold, italic, or underline in all keywords contained in the article, because doing so would indicate abnormality, and Google would assume that such a technique was applied in order to manipulate the crawler. Three style-emphasized words and three special headings with different font size should be enough to emphasize on certain things in your article.

So, select the first keyword in your article and apply the bold style, using the WordPress article toolbar. Accordingly, continue with the styles italic and underline. Then select three headings embedded in the article and apply the styles H1, H2, H3 accordingly, from the article toolbar *(Figure 5-5)*.

In addition, make the first keyword of your article a link itself, leading to an external page, as Google likes websites that link to each other and work as reference to one another, a key ingredient in SEO.

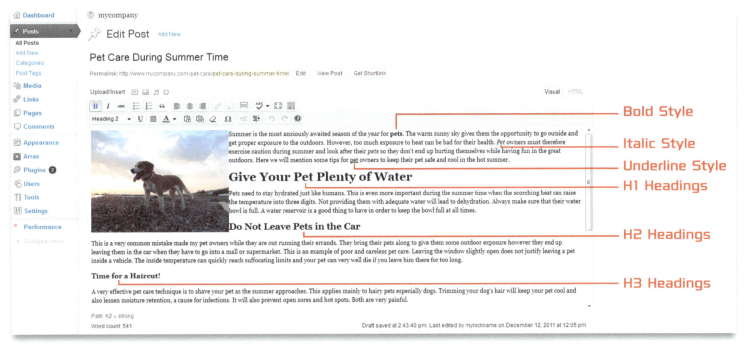

FIGURE 5-5

Now that you are done emphasizing the keywords and the main titles, you will proceed with the addition of an internal link to the article you are working on. Select and copy the article's URL, as is, next to the word *"permalink,"* which is found under your article's title. Then select the first keyword in your article and press *"Insert/ Edit Link" button* 🔗 from the WordPress article toolbar, to insert the URL. Paste the article's URL in the pop-up window that appears right after pressing the "Insert/Edit Link" button 🔗 , and press **Add Link** *(Figure 5-6)*. Do not forget to write a title for the link. Finally, press **Update** to apply the changes *(Figure 5-7)*.

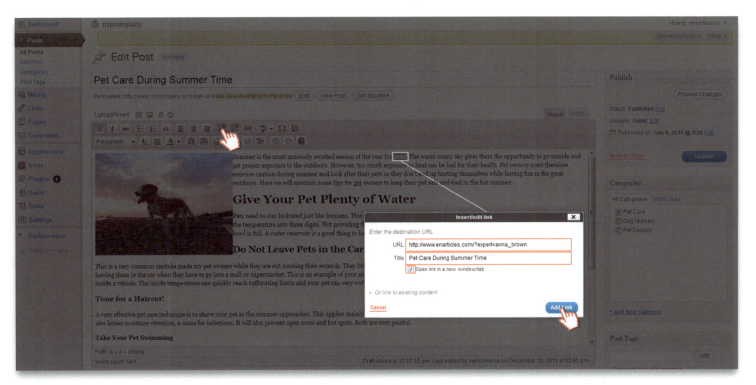

FIGURE 5-6

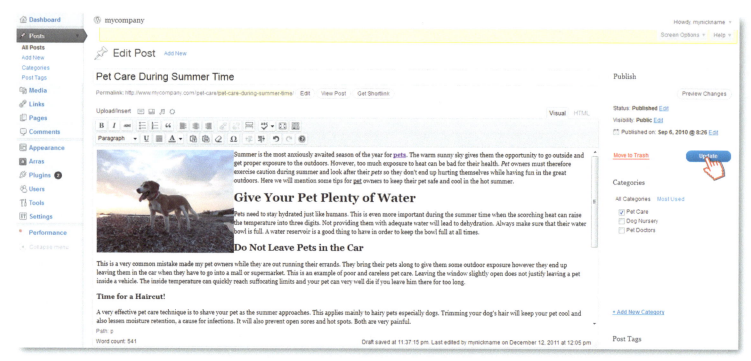

FIGURE 5-7

Adding Keywords to Images

You can apply advanced SEO techniques not only in the main text body, but also in the images. In addition to the SEO techniques applied in the previous chapters, you can also make your images even more Google-friendly, in order to enhance the overall SEO strategy of your website. If your articles contain no images, you 'd better add at least one to each article, not only to make them more attractive to your potential readers but also to prepare the ground for another SEO technique. To insert an image, first choose the article you want to process, place your pointer inside the exact line of the body text where the image will be inserted, and then press the Upload/Insert   button on the WordPress post toolbar (Figure 5-8).

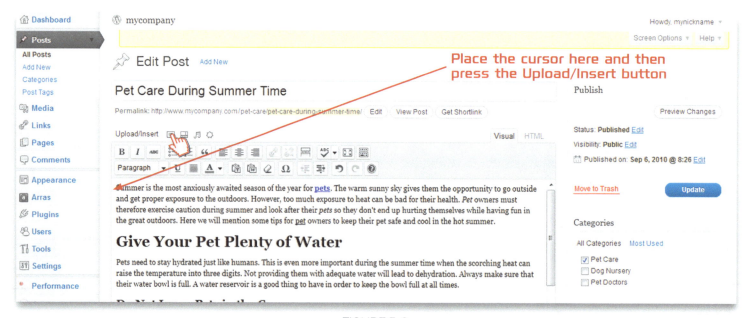

FIGURE 5-8

After that, press the Select Files button on the pop-up window that shows up and browse the appropriate image. Once the image is uploaded by WordPress, you will be able to see it in the pop-up window; then look for the fields *"Title", "Alternate Text", "Description"* and fill them with keywords related to your article. In the example used here, I simply inserted the title of the article, just because it is expressed in keywords. If you are lazy, like me, you can do so, as well. Then, press the Insert into Post button to insert the image in the article *(Figure 5-9)*.

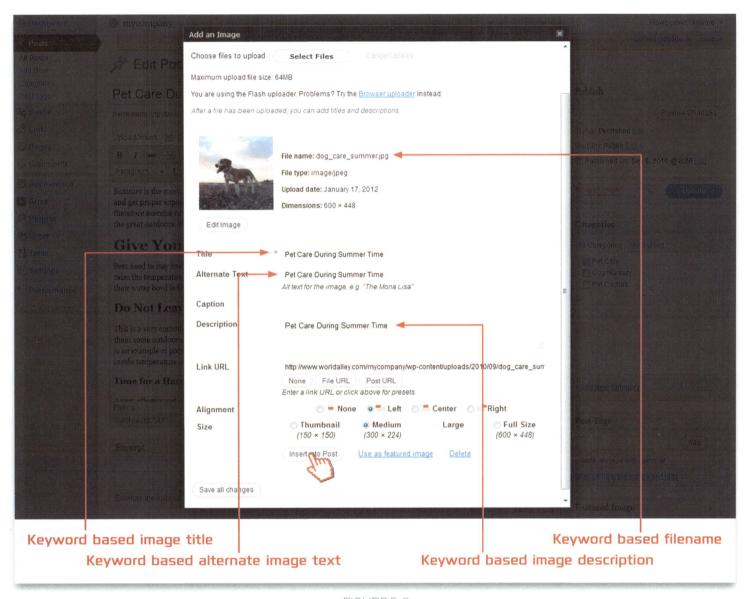

FIGURE 5-9

Finally, press Update to save the changes you have made. Should you want the image to appear in larger dimensions, or on the right side of the text, you can edit it by selecting it and pressing the *"Edit Image"* button that appears on it.

Advanced Creation Techniques for SEO Static Pages

Creating Static Pages

In this chapter you will learn how to create SEO-ready static pages. I will show you how to apply basic and advanced SEO techniques on page titles, permalinks, and even on WordPress header.php file.

Page Title

Select *"Add New"* to create a new page and fill in the title of your static page, using keywords in accordance to the page. Try to avoid the commonly used phrases, such as *"about"* for information concerning your company or *"contact"* for information such as your email address and company location. So, the right way to do this is by including 2 to 3 keywords in the page title, such as *"about dog care"* or *"contact dog care center."* This way, you make your website even more intriguing to the search engine.

Page Permalinks

After you have written the page title, the permalink URL will appear underneath it. Press the Edit button and rewrite the permalink's URL. Now change the URL so that it includes the same keywords you previously used in the static page title. Do not forget to separate the words with hyphens. Remember not to use spaces between the words. If you have already applied the suggested settings mentioned in Chapter 2 regarding the proper use of the permalinks, then the URL will automatically take the desired form.

Page Main Content

This is where you type the main body text of your static page. Try to maximize the use of keywords relevant to the content of the page. The keywords must be used in a way that the text is syntactically correct and makes sense to the reader. The excessive and meaningless use of keywords brings down the level of importance of your website, as Google realizes that you are trying to manipulate the search engine and as a result, your website does not appear on the first pages of the Google results page.

Advanced Page Title SEO Technique

In this section, I will show you how to make all page headers even more attractive and Google friendly.

Advanced Web Page Title

A web page title is the title that appears on the top of the web browser, such as Internet Explorer or Firefox. It is also the underlined phrase in blue letters that appears on the Google search results page *(Figure 6-1 , 6-2)*.

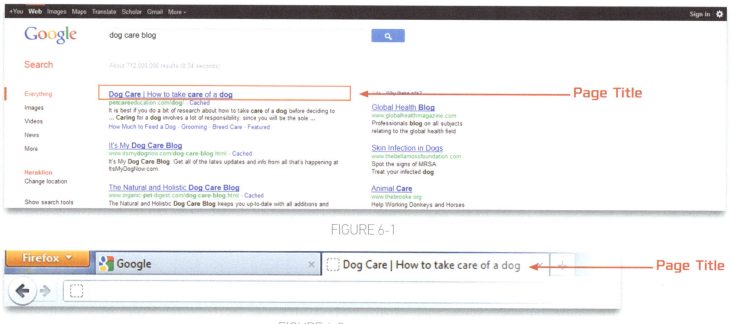

FIGURE 6-1

FIGURE 6-2

The choice of your title is far too important, because this is in fact the first thing that Google "sees" when it crawls your website. The appearance of the title can be adjusted from WordPress's Dashboard, by selecting General Settings and then Site title. Both of these have already been thoroughly explained in Chapters 2. The title that appears on your homepage is the one you have already filled in at WordPress General Settings. This is what your visitors actually see when your homepage is being loaded on the browser. However, when a static page or an article page is loaded, the homepage title is replaced by the article's/static page's title. The ideal solution would be to have both the homepage title and the article's/static page's title appearing at the same time, not only for the users' eyes to see but also for Google. This is because the Google search engine indexes WordPress articles as unique pages. All article titles are based on keywords. So, if during a user's search query, Google matches the words requested with the keywords of your article's title, it then lists your website on the search results page. As you can easily see, if both the homepage title and the article title were embedded in every single page, then more keywords would be available for Google to match, leading to higher chances of a better placement on the Google results page.

So, for the two different titles to appear simultaneously on each and every page, you must add a line of code in the WordPress file header.php. This can be done in two ways: either by downloading the file with an FTP client and then editing it, or by using the WordPress control panel. In the second case, which is far easier, go to *"Appearance"* -> *"Editor"* and then select *"Header"* on the right section of the screen *(header.php)*. Then look for the code line starting with the command <title> and ending with the command </title> *(Figure 6-3)*, and replace the entire line with the following php code *(Figure 6-4)*.

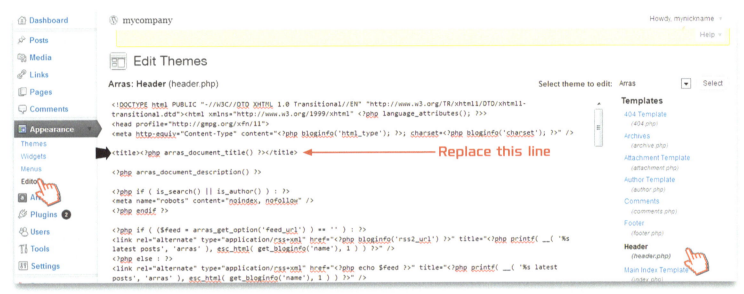

FIGURE 6-3

```
<title><?php wp_title(''); ?><?php if(wp_title('', false)) { echo ' :: '; }
?><?php bloginfo('name'); ?></title>
```

FIGURE 6-4

Finally press the [Update File] button, to save the changes *(Figure 6-5)*.

FIGURE 6-5

SEO Plugins & Files You Must Have

Plugins are small additional scripts made to perform specific tasks in the background and function in a supportive way, by enriching the WordPress platform with new capabilities. They are easy to use, because you only have to install them, activate them, and make the necessary adjustments in order for them to work, without any further future actions. There are many different plugins built to perform various tasks; however, you will only deal with the ones that help you promote your website in the best possible way.

Google XML Sitemaps Plugin
So, what is this xml sitemap?

In a website, not all pages are connected to each other. When the crawler reads the content of a page, it locates all the internal links contained in it. But what about the links of other pages that are not created within WordPress, yet are contained in your website? The answer to this problem is called sitemap XML. The XML sitemap is actually the file that includes every internal link of articles and static pages contained in your website. The XML sitemap is one of the most important parts of today's Google-friendly websites. The reason for this is because Google has created a specific webpage for Webmasters to submit the sitemap of the website they have created, called "Webmaster Tools," which is located at https://www.google.com/webmasters/tools/. A more detailed description of Google's Webmaster Tools is given in Chapter 8.

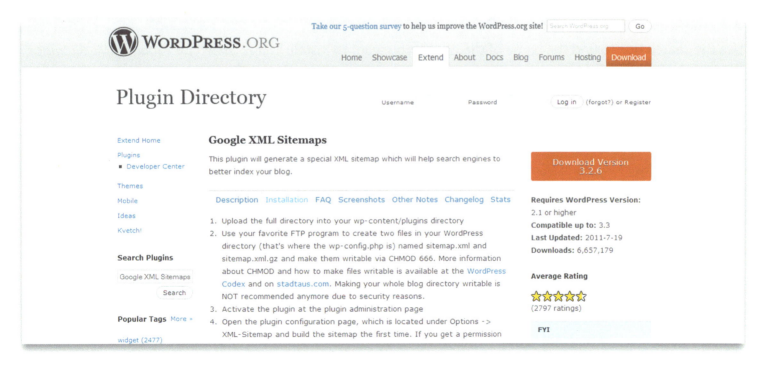

So Google reads the XML sitemap and the articles that correspond to the links, and indexes them in its database. This way, not only does Google need less time to crawl your website for new links, but you as well are able to emphasize on the most noteworthy articles. At the same time, Google uses your XML sitemap in order to enlist your links, based on your own testimonies, without having to search your website again and again for new links.

The True Power of Google XML Sitemaps Plugin

The true power of the sitemap plugin is that it automates all procedures regarding the creation and publication of the sitemap. Once activated, it creates the sitemap of your website. It then informs Google and other search engines, like Bing and Yahoo about the publication of the new sitemap. When you post a new article, the plugin creates a newly updated version of the *sitemap.xml* file. This file contains the link to your new article and also informs Google about the new version of the sitemap.xml file, so that the search engine crawls the file in order to "see" and index the new link. All of the previously mentioned actions take place automatically, as soon as you press *"Publish,"* after you are done writing your article. Links to static pages, categories, tags, authors, and archives can also be included in the sitemap, some of them manually.

Google XML Sitemaps Plugin Installation

WordPress plugins can be installed in two ways. Firstly, they can be uploaded to the plugins directory, which is located at the web server in WordPress Installation, using an FTP client. Secondly, a much easier way is to use the WordPress control panel—and so will I, in the following tutorial.

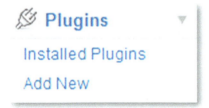

Use the search box to find the name of the plugin you want to install; in this case type *"Google XML Sitemaps"* and press the Search Plugins button *(Figure 7-1)*.

FIGURE 7-1

In the list of plugins, look for the specific plugin you requested (usually listed on the very top). When you find it, press the *"Install Now"* link under the plugin's name *(Figure 7-2)*.

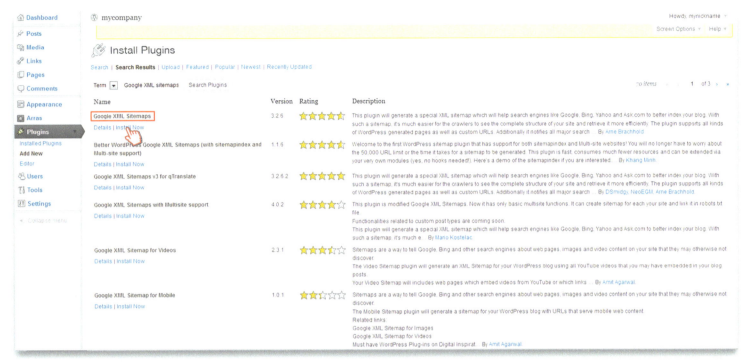

FIGURE 7-2

A pop-up window then appears, asking you, *"Are you sure you want to install this plugin?"* Just press the OK button to continue *(Figure 7-3)*.

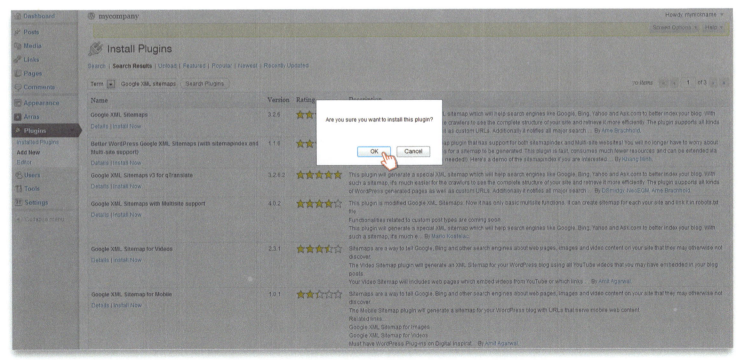

FIGURE 7-3

In the screen following the plugin installation, press the *"Activate Plugin"* link *(Figure 7-4)*.

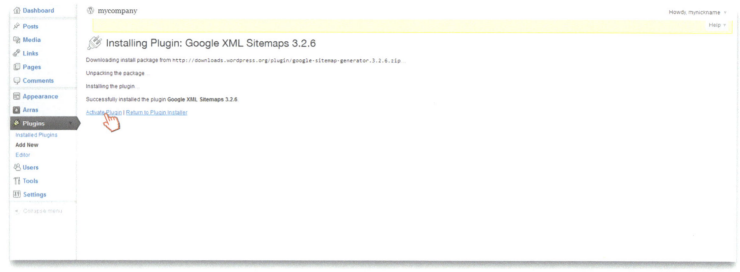

FIGURE 7-4

Then go to WordPress General Settings, where a new option is available called *"XML Sitemap" (Figure 7-5)*. Click on it to make the necessary adjustments for the plugin to meet your specific needs. In general, default settings work just fine for an average user.

FIGURE 7-5

All you need to do is to create the sitemap for the first time manually, just by pressing the *"Click here"* link on the sentence *"The sitemap wasn't built yet. Click here to build it the first time" (Figure 7-6)*.

FIGURE 7-6

After that, you can adjust the plugin so as to meet your website's needs, by carefully reading the plugin settings page. For example, you can include static pages or exclude some categories from the sitemap. You can even add pages to the XML sitemap that have not been built with the use of WordPress CMS but have been added to the website manually. However, the default settings are quite sufficient for most users *(Figure 7-7)*.

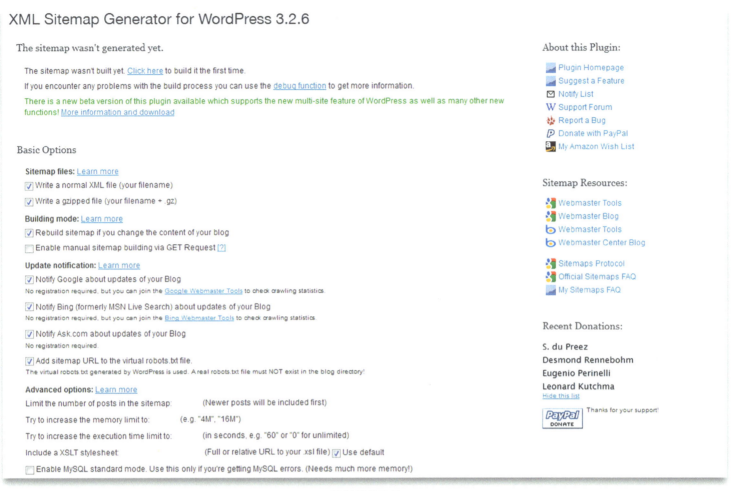

FIGURE 7-7

Here are the basic key selections that must be enabled on the XML Sitemap Generator options page:

☑ Write a normal XML file (your filename)

By selecting this option you enable the plugin to name the sitemap with the default file name which is *sitemap.xml. These is no need to name the sitemap.xml by yourself.*

☑ Write a gzipped file (your filename + .gz)

By selecting this option you enable the plugin to create a compressed version of the sitemap.xml file. Usually the compressed version of the *sitemap.xml* is required by the *robots.txt* file.

☑ Rebuild sitemap if you change the content of your blog

This is one of the most important options of the plugin. Once you enable this option, everytime you create a new post on your website, the plugin rebuilds the sitemap.xml file automatically.

☑ Notify Google about updates of your Blog
No registration required, but you can join the Google Webmaster Tools to check crawling statistics.

Here is another important option of the plugin. Everytime the sitemap.xml file is rebuilt, the plugin notifies Google on the updated version of the sitemap.xml file, so that Google may access its content and index any new reference to fresh, published material.

☑ Notify Bing (formerly MSN Live Search) about updates of your Blog
No registration required, but you can join the Bing Webmaster Tools to check crawling statistics.

☑ Notify Ask.com about updates of your Blog
No registration required.

The plugin also notifies Microsoft's Bing Search Engine and Ask.com on all changes made to the *sitemap.xml* file. Always bear in mind that all traffic is good, whichever the source of origin.

☑ Add sitemap URL to the virtual robots.txt file.
The virtual robots.txt generated by WordPress is used. A real robots.txt file must NOT exist in the blog directory!

This option enables the plugin to insert the compressed version of sitemam.xml file into the robots.txt file.

Sitemap Content

WordPress standard content:
☑ Include homepage
☑ Include posts
☐ Include following pages of multi-page posts (Increases build time and memory usage!)
☑ Include static pages

By selecting these options you allow the plugin to include Homepage, Posts and Static pages to the *sitemap.xml* file. If you select more options, such as categories, archives, tag pages, you risk losing your high position in Google ranking, because of the content duplication.

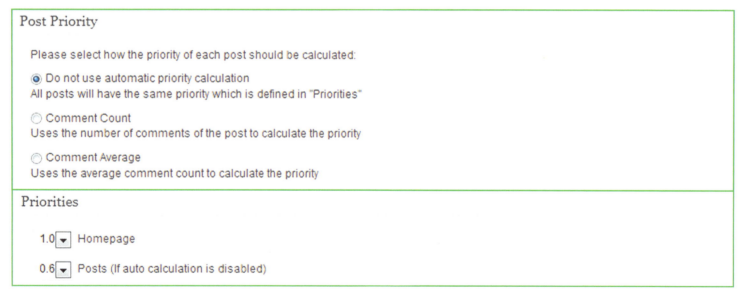

Post Priority

Please select how the priority of each post should be calculated:
◉ Do not use automatic priority calculation
All posts will have the same priority which is defined in "Priorities"

◯ Comment Count
Uses the number of comments of the post to calculate the priority

◯ Comment Average
Uses the average comment count to calculate the priority

Priorities

1.0 ▼ Homepage

0.6 ▼ Posts (If auto calculation is disabled)

Choose *"Do not use automatic priority calculation",* in order to prioritize entries of new posts manually, by adjusting the priority level numerically, from the priorities menu at the end of the plugin's options page. Choose the priority level of each content category, based on the frequency by which you update each one of them. When you are done with the settings, just press the (Update options) button to rebuild the sitemap. From now on, your website has a complete, accurate, and Google-friendly XML sitemap, located at *http://www.mycompany.com/sitemap.xml*. Most importantly, you now have a sitemap that is automatically updated whenever you add a new article, and that informs Google every time its content changes.

iRobots.txt SEO Plugin

So, what is this iRobots.txt SEO Plugin ?

Robots.txt is a guideline file, helpful to Google. WordPress contains many folders that are not necessarily worth-indexed during the crawling procedure, such as the wp-admin folder that contains all the administration files required by WordPress and is of zero importance to Google and its searchers. With the use of *robots.txt*, you avoid indexing unnecessary content.

Another reason why you must create robots.txt is because it prevents the Google search engine from reaching the same content from more than one location. This may happen when you post a new article that appears on all of the following three—the category folder, the monthly archives, and the particular tag. Google hates content duplication and punishes your website by ranking it down. A *robots.txt* file increases the efficiency of the Google crawler, and that's great for SEO. In fact, what a *robots.txt* file does is to create a guideline that allows or disallows search bots to have access to folders.

iRobots.txt SEO Plugin Installation

To install the **iRobots.txt SEO** plugin, go to the plugins management menu and select "Add New." In the search box that will then appear, type the full name of the plugin, which is *"iRobots.txt SEO"* and then press the [Search Plugins] button *(Figure 7-8)*.

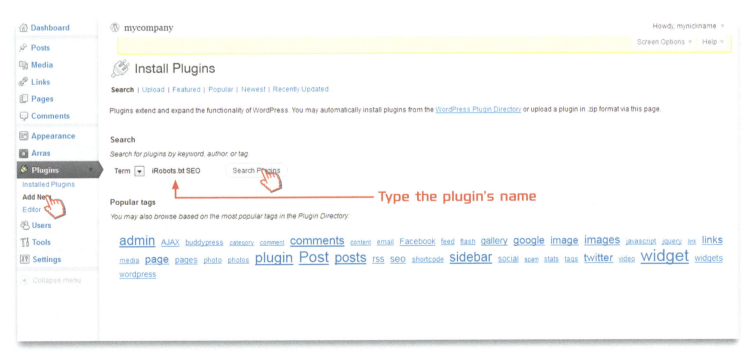

FIGURE 7-8

In the list of plugins, look for the specific plugin you requested (usually listed on the very top). When you find it, press the *"Install Now"* link under the plugin's name *(Figure 7-9)*.

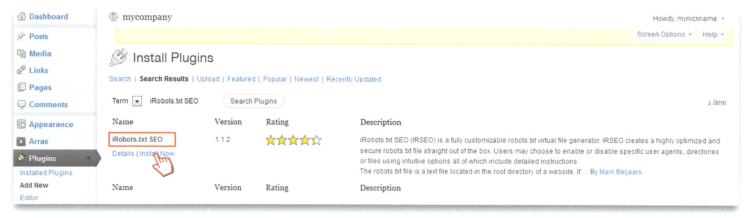

FIGURE 7-9

A pop-up window then appears, asking you, *"Are you sure you want to install this plugin?"*
Just press the [OK] button to continue *(Figure 7-10)*.

FIGURE 7-10

On the next screen, the plugin informs you that the operation is complete, and you must press the *"Activate Plugin"* link under the plugin's name to make the plugin work *(Figure 7-11)*.

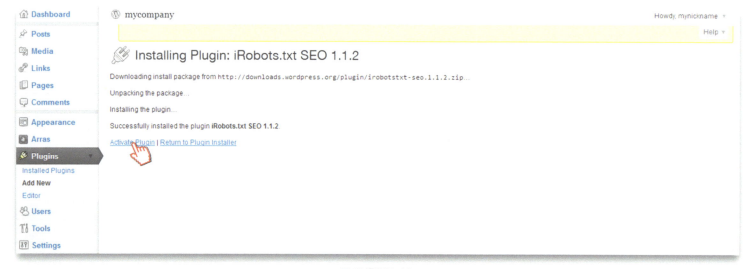

FIGURE 7-11

Then go to WordPress General Settings, where a new option is available called *"iRobots.txt SEO."* Click on it to make the necessary adjustments *(Figure 7-12)*.

FIGURE 7-12

In general, default settings work just fine for an average user. All you need to do is to create the *robots.txt* file for the first time manually, just by pressing the ⟨ Update options ⟩ button *(Figure 7-13)* . Note that **iRobots.txt SEO** plugin creates a virtual *robots.txt* file which is hidden inside your server. This *robots.txt file* is displayed whenever access to the *robots.txt* file is requested.

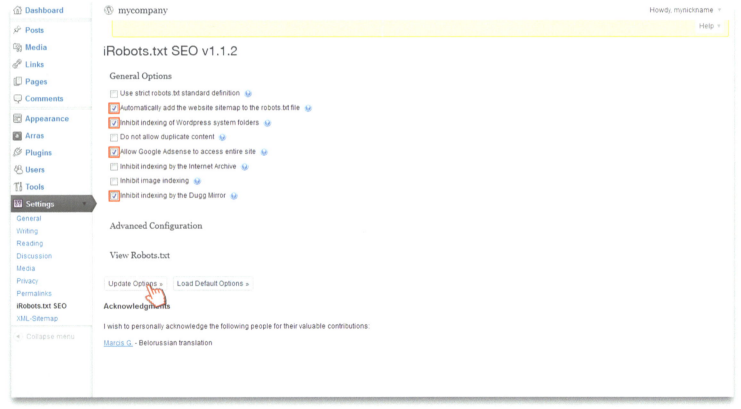

FIGURE 7-13

Your website now has a robots.txt file, which is Google friendly and SEO optimized. The next time that the Google crawler passes by your website, it will locate the *robots.txt* file and it will read your website's content based on it's new guidelines provided by the file. This way your website will be greatly appreciated by Google, because by using *robots.txt* you are kindly showing Google which content it should take and what to ignore. This gives your website an advantage against your competitors and a better ranking in SERP.

Using Google's Webmaster Tools Like a Superhero

In the previous chapters, you have laid the necessary foundations which enable you to submit your website properly to Google. By following my instructions step-by-step, you have successfully created an entirely Google-friendly website. Now is the right time to show Google what a great job you have done by precisely following its guidelines. By using Google Webmaster Tools, you can show the search engine the exact location of your website, its sitemap, and the *robots.txt* file, so that the Google crawler may start visiting it and indexing your pages in its database.

Google Webmaster Tools

Open your favorite web browser and just type in the Webmaster Tools URL, which is :

https://www.google.com/webmasters/tools/

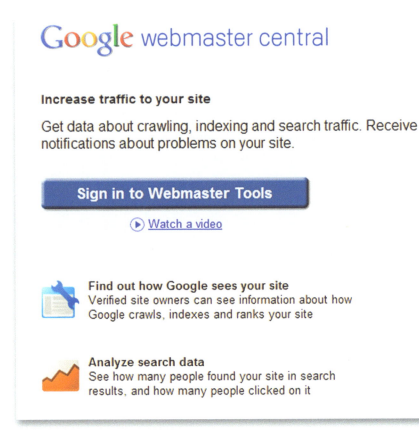

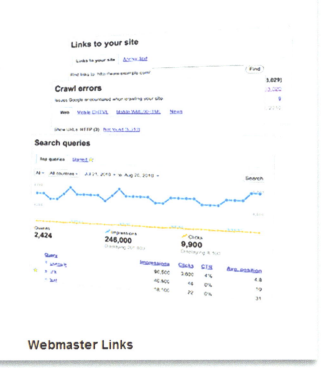

You will then be redirected to the homepage of the tools, which is actually the login page *(Figure 8-1)*. Firstly, you must create an account with Google, in case you don't already own one. If you do have an email account with Google, you are good to go. Just log in to Google Webmaster Tools with the credentials you use when you log in to your Gmail account. You only need one valid account to access all Google services and goodies, such as *AdWords, AdSense, etc.*

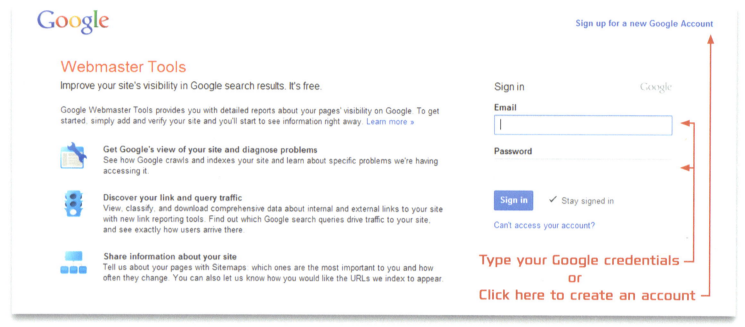

FIGURE 8-1

After logging in, you are redirected to the tools dashboard. Click on the ADD A SITE button found in the right of the screen, fill in your domain name *(e.g. www.mycompany.com)*, and press the Continue button *(Figure 8-2)*.

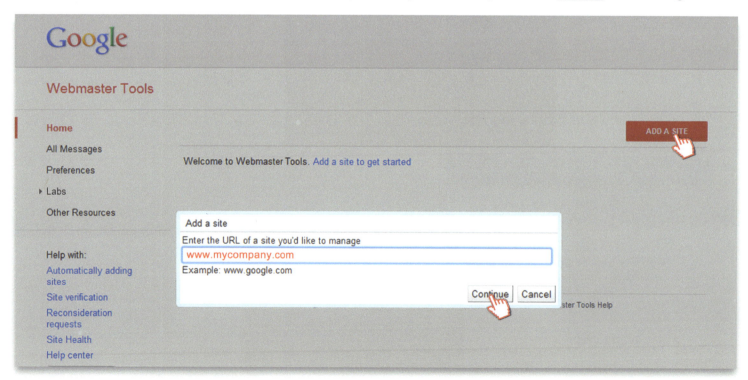

FIGURE 8-2

Verify Ownership

On the next screen, you will be asked to *"Verify Ownership"* of your website by choosing one of four methods. The easiest and most reliable one is the first on the list, which uses meta tags. This is easiest because you can copy the line of the verification code provided by Google, and paste it directly to your theme's header using the—well-known by now—WordPress administration panel, compared to other more advanced ways such as uploading a file to your server, modifying the DNS servers, or using Google Analytics. Meta tags will be inserted in the current theme of your WordPress website. If you change your website theme, you must repeat the same process all over again. Select *"Add meta tag to your site's homepage."* Copy the meta tag line of code *(Figure 8-3)*.

> Note: If you change your website theme, you must repeat the following process all over again.

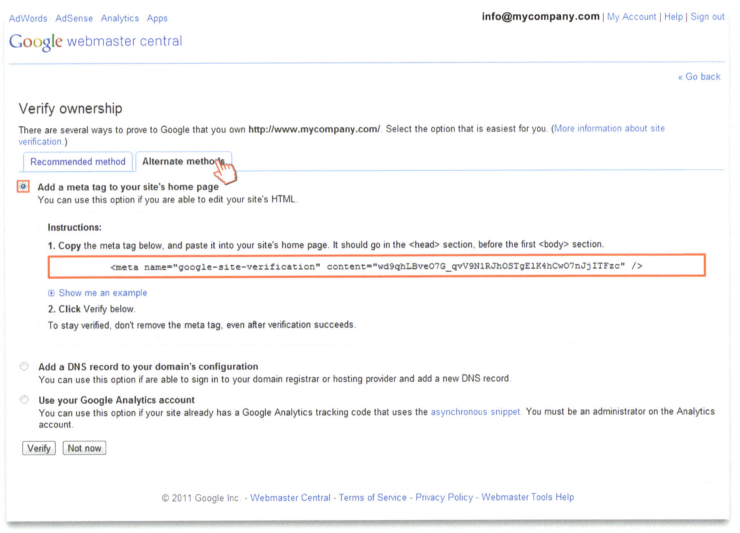

FIGURE 8-3

Leave the current browser page as it is, and open a new tab on the browser in order to load the WordPress administrator panel. **Do not press the** Verify **button yet.**

To add the meta tag line of code that you previously copied, go to *"Appearance Menu"* -> *"Editor"* and select the file header.php, located on the right side of the screen. Then, paste the meta tag line of code to the meta tags section of the header.php file. The meta tag line of code must be inserted somewhere between <head> and </head>. What you must ensure is that the line of code is inserted into an empty line *(Figure 8-4)*. Finally, press the **Update File** button to apply the changes.

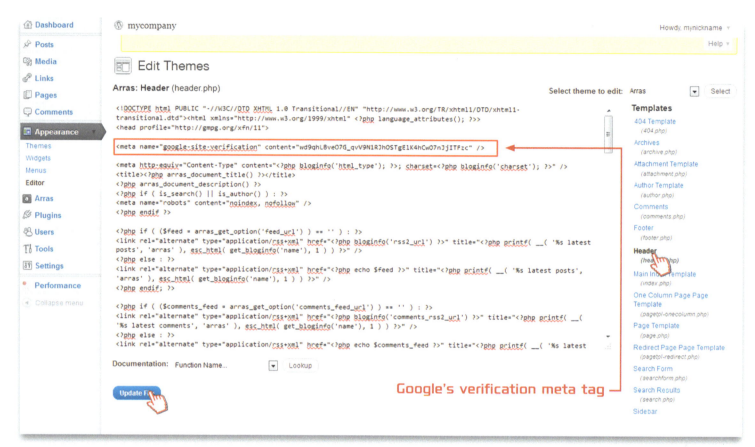

FIGURE 8-4

Now go back to the previous tab of the browser where you have been working on the Google Webmaster Tools, and press the Verify button *(Figure 8-5)*. The verification process of your website is now complete. From now on, Google can easily verify the existence and the functionality of your website anytime.

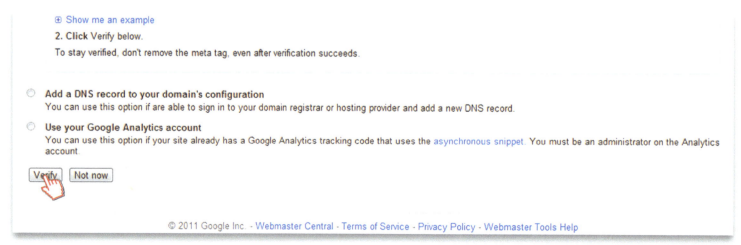

FIGURE 8-5

Submitting Your Sitemap.xml to Google

Having completed the verification process, you are now transferred to the Management Dashboard. At this point, you will publish the sitemap of your website by doing the following:

 Make sure that you are at the management section of your website and not at the homepage of the Webmaster Tools. In order to navigate to the management section of your website, just click on the domain name, which is displayed below the headline *"Sites"* on the homepage of the Webmaster Tools.

 On the left side of the Dashboard screen, select *"Site Configuration"* and then *"Sitemaps."* Press the Submit a Sitemap button and fill in the name of the file *sitemap.xml* and then press the Submit Sitemap button to publish the file *(Figure 8-6)*.

Congratulations! You have now successfully submitted your website's sitemap to Google.

FIGURE 8-6

In the following (status) screen, notice the small check mark that now appears and the fields *"URLs submitted"* , *currently filled in with the number 5* and *"URLs in web index"* which is currently empty *(Figure 8-7)*.

FIGURE 8-7

This happens because on the one hand Google is informed of the existence of your sitemap, but on the other hand the Google crawler has not accessed its content yet. It usually takes 1 to 2 hours for the Google crawler to access the content of your sitemap. When the crawler finally does access it, the exact number of your links contained in your sitemap will then appear under the header *"URLs Submitted."* The links indexed in the database of the search engine will appear under the header *"URLs in Web Index."* It takes a while for all the URLs contained in your sitemap to be indexed, but as time goes by, Google will find interest in an increasing number of links in your website that are worth-indexed in the search engine.

Checking Robots.txt Status

The crawler access page gives you all the information regarding the access status that the Google crawler has on the *sitemap.xml* and the *robots.txt* files *(Figure 8-8)*. This way you can submit your website's sitemap and follow up on the *robots.txt* status. Both of these submissions help you get a higher ranking in the search results page, opening the road to success. What is more, by using Google Webmaster Tools you have access to numerous statistical data about your website's keywords popularity and many other things. It is highly suggested that you use them, in order to better understand the way in which the search engine actually works and to observe the behavior of your potential visitors.

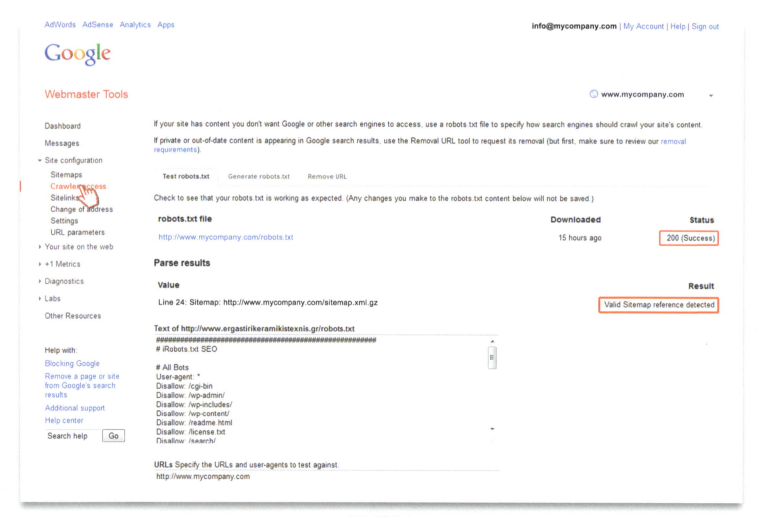

FIGURE 8-8

Site Performance

On the Google Webmaster tools menu, you can find a section called *"Labs,"* which contains five more tools: the Author stats, the Custom Search, the Instant previews, the Video Sitemaps, and the Site performance that will be extensively described in the next chapter *(Figure 8-9)*.

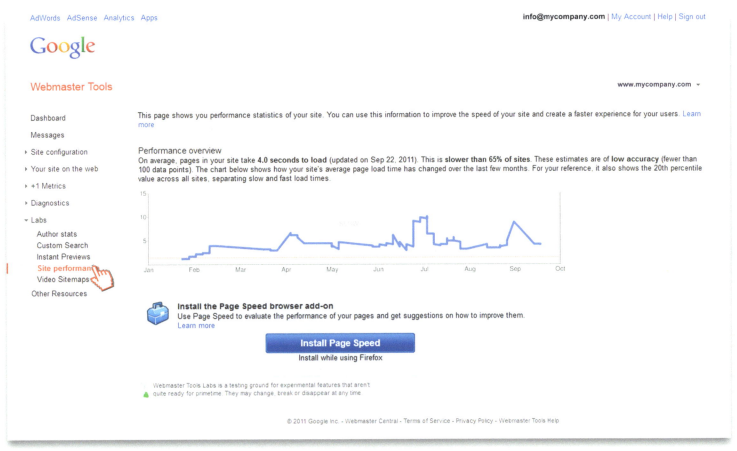

FIGURE 8-9

Site Speed Is More Than a Future SEO Ranking Factor

Let's suppose that there are two different websites that contain relatively similar content. However, one of them requires more time to be loaded in the browser window. In which one do you think the visitor will in fact access more content? The answer is actually quite obvious. Websites that take less time to load have an edge against all others, because the user can browse more content in his or her limited available time, also making the browsing a pleasant experience. Browsing a website should be like turning the pages of a magazine. The user should be able to jump from one page to another, with

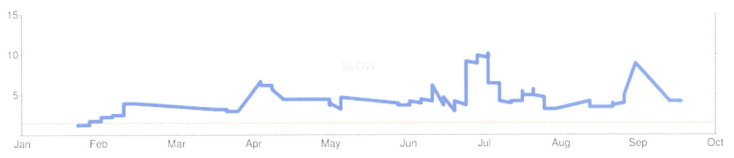

no delay, in order to read more content, or review more products. By going from one page to another faster, the visitor spends more time in your website and therefore sees more content or products. So, it is more likely that the visitor will turn into a potential buyer.

Another reason why a website must load faster is also mentioned in an article by Matt Cutts, one of the top SEO specialists. In his article, it is suggested that a page's load time may be a significant page-ranking factor, because Google's Webmaster Tools actually measure the time required for a website to be loaded by one's browser, compared to all other websites submitted to Google. However, the above-mentioned argument is still to be proved. It is a solid fact that Google has already started measuring the page load time for all verified websites. So an increasing number of Webmasters are working on the improvement of the page load time, so that they are well prepared against their competitors, in case Google actually does take page-loading speed as an SEO factor.

In this chapter, I will show you the three most effective ways to improve the performance of your website in terms of loading speed: page and content caching, content delivery network, and reduced image size.

Let's Start With Some Fundamental Speed Rules

Keep your WordPress version up-to-date.

Each new version of WordPress contains numerous improvements. Every new release is in fact an effort made by the developers to increase WordPress's speed and safety. That's why you must always upgrade to the latest WordPress version, to get the performance improvements and all the new features.

Do not keep inactive plugins.

Most WordPress webmasters try out new plugins to add extra features to their websites. However, if these do not deliver the expected results, the webmasters simply deactivate them. Though deactivated, the plugins increase the page load time, as several queries have already been inserted to either the WordPress database or the template. You must also keep an eye on the plugins that have been activated but not put in use, because these not only affect the page load time, but also may consume valuable resources, resulting in web server overload (Error 500 page). So try to keep the plugin directory clean and tidy. If you feel that you might want to use those deactivated plugins later on, then make a text document with the list of plugins you will need later, and you can safely delete the ones that are not needed now.

Disable Hotlinking.

Stealing bandwidth from your website is an act called hotlinking. This happens when other websites link to articles and images contained in your website, loaded from your server. In fact, they are actually not hosting images and articles on their own server, but they are transferring them from yours. This practice reduces your available bandwidth, because if thousands of different websites are loading images from your server, then there will be no available bandwidth left for your visitors to use. The solution to this problem is quite easy. Simply disable hotlinking from your server's cPanel (Figure 9-1). On the next screen *(Figure 9-2)* you must Block direct access to specific file types.

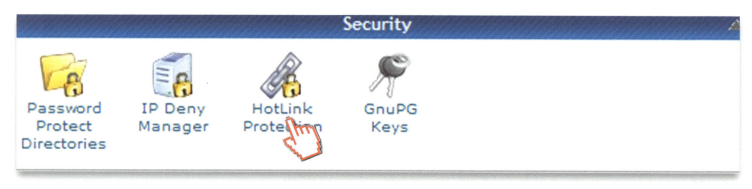

FIGURE 9-1

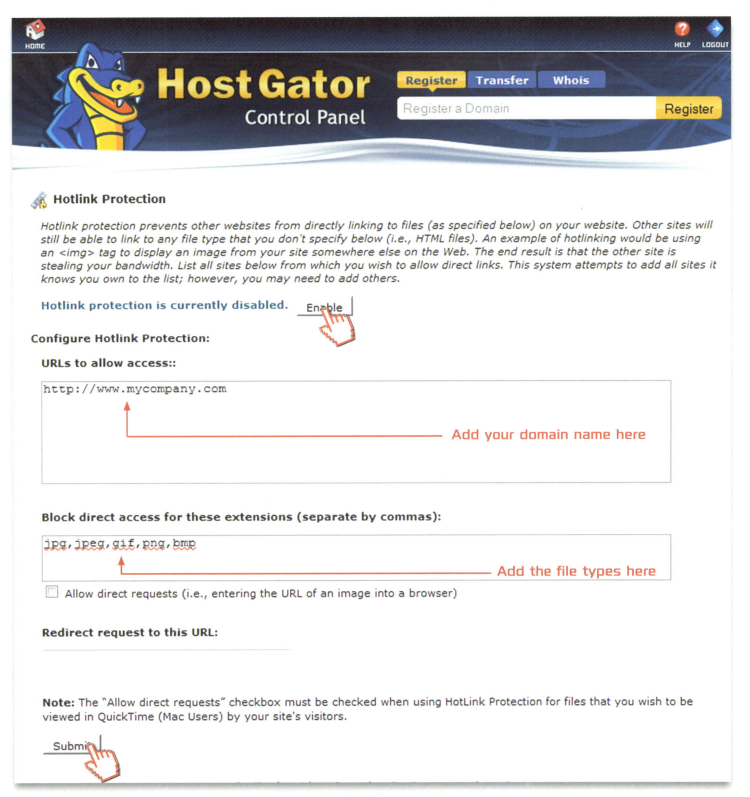

FIGURE 9-2

Adding Restriction to the .htaccess File

In case your web server does not support cPanel, you will have to add some restrictions to the .htaccess file, in order to disable hotlinking . To do so, you must edit the .htaccess file, using, your favorite by now, ftp client. To edit the .htaccess file you need to access the root folder of your web server and edit it as follow. Transfer the .htaccess file from the web server to your computer and open it, using a text editor. Once you open your .htaccess file, you will find some code already present in it, created by the initial WordPress installation procedure. Please do not touch any part of that code, as it contains the default settings that are required by WordPress permalink structures. A back up version of the original .htaccess file must be saved before you make any changes. Here is the default WordPress code for your reference:

```
# BEGIN WordPress
<IfModule mod_rewrite.c>
RewriteEngine On
RewriteBase /
RewriteRule ^index\.php$ - [L]
RewriteCond %{REQUEST_FILENAME} !-f
RewriteCond %{REQUEST_FILENAME} !-d
RewriteRule . /index.php [L]
</IfModule>
# END WordPress
```

Hot Linking protection code

Now, in order to prevent hot linking of images and other file types, add the following code inside the existing .htaccess file under the last line of code. Remember to replace *"mycompany.com"* with your own domain. The following code creates a failed request when hot linking to file types such as gif, jpg, js and css is attempted.

```
RewriteEngine on
RewriteCond %{HTTP_REFERER} !^$
RewriteCond %{HTTP_REFERER} !^http://(www\.)?mycompany.com/.*$ [NC]
RewriteRule \.(gif|jpg|js|css)$ - [F]
```

WordPress modified .htaccess file with hot linking protection

Here is the modified version of the Wordpress .htaccess file that includes hot linking protection.

```
# BEGIN WordPress
<IfModule mod_rewrite.c>
RewriteEngine On
RewriteBase /
RewriteRule ^index\.php$ - [L]
RewriteCond %{REQUEST_FILENAME} !-f
RewriteCond %{REQUEST_FILENAME} !-d
RewriteRule . /index.php [L]
</IfModule>
# END WordPress
RewriteEngine on
RewriteCond %{HTTP_REFERER} !^$
RewriteCond %{HTTP_REFERER} !^http://(www\.)?mycompany.com/.*$ [NC]
RewriteRule \.(gif|jpg|js|css)$ - [F]
```

Finally upload the new .htaccess file to the root folder of your web server and replace the old one.

Website Speed Measurement Tools

To improve your load speed time, you must firstly be aware of the current load speed time. This way, you can easily compare and quantify the improvements on the load speed time, after having applied the following tips. To obtain an accurate speed load time measurement, you will need to install an add-on to the Firefox web browser, called **YSlow,** which is made by Yahoo developers. YSlow displays the page load time on the bottom right side of the browser in the add-on bar. What is more, it provides you with extensive data regarding the rating of your website in terms of load speed time, and it informs you on the factors that decrease its performance. YSlow for Firefox runs in the **Firebug** add-on window, so in order to run the tool, the Firebug add-on must be installed and enabled.

Installing add-ons for Firefox Browser

Navigate to firefox browser menu and locate the add-ons button *(Figure 9-3)*.

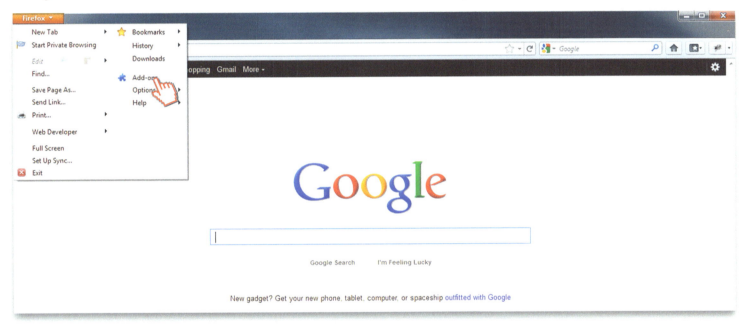

FIGURE 9-3

Installing Firebug add-on for Firefox Browser

Type *"firebug"* in the search box and press enter to find the specific add-on. Then press the ⬚Install⬚ button to complete the add-on installation process *(Figure 9-4)*. Restart Firefox.

FIGURE 9-4

Installing YSlow add-on for Firefox Browser

Type *"YSlow"* in the search box and press enter to find the specific add-on. Then press the Install button to complete the add-on installation process *(Figure 9-5)*. Restart Firefox.

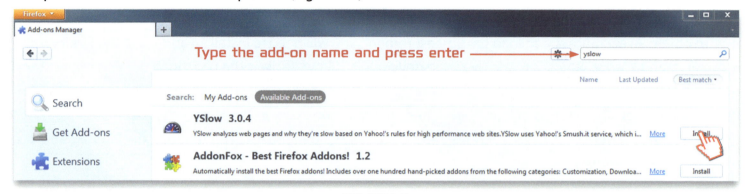

FIGURE 9-5

Checking Firebug and YSlow status

First load your website on firefox browser and press the firebug button on the top right corner of Firefox to open the firebug window. Then locate the YSlow button in order to run the speed test *(Figure 9-6)*.

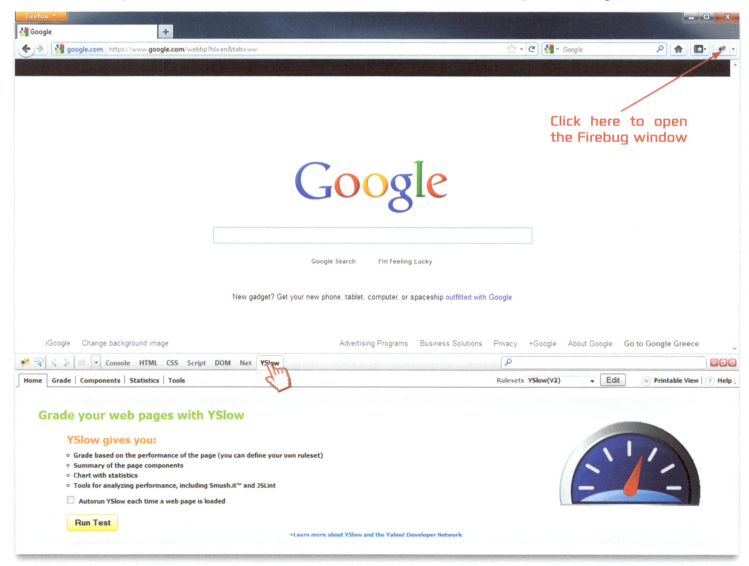

FIGURE 9-6

Page and Content Caching

A web cache is a mechanism of temporary storage of a website's content, such as HTML pages and images, helping you to reduce bandwidth usage and server load. When visiting a website that uses a web cache mechanism, the content of the website is not called from the database in real time, but is loaded from the temporary storage of the web cache. So the content displayed on the browser is a previously stored version of the website. This way, the load speed time is significantly reduced. In WordPress you can apply page and content caching by using the W3 Total Cache Plugin.

W3 Total Cache Plugin

The W3 Total Cache plugin improves the user experience of your website by improving your server performance, caching every aspect of your site, reducing the download times, and providing transparent content delivery network (CDN) integration. Specifically, its use includes the following benefits and features.

Benefits:

- At least 10x improvement in overall site performance (Grade A in YSlow or significant Google Page Speed improvements) when fully configured
- Improved conversion rates and site performance which affect your site's rank on Google
- Instant subsequent page views: browser caching
- Optimized progressive render : pages start rendering quickly
- Reduced page load time: increased visitor time on site; visitors view more pages
- Improved web server performance; sustains high traffic periods
- Up to 80% bandwidth savings via minify and HTTP compression of HTML, CSS, JavaScript, and feeds

Features:

- Compatible with shared hosting, virtual private/dedicated servers, and dedicated servers/clusters
- Transparent CDN integration with Media Library , theme files, and WordPress itself
- Mobile support: respective caching of pages by referrer or groups of user agents including theme switch-
- ing for groups of referrers or user agents
- Caching of (minified and compressed) pages and posts in memory or on disk or on CDN (mirror only)
- Caching of (minified and compressed) CSS and JavaScript in memory, on disk, or on CDN
- Caching of feeds (site, categories, tags, comments, search results) in memory or on disk or on CDN (mirror only)
- Caching of search results pages (i.e. URLs with query string variables) in memory or on disk
- Caching of database objects in memory or on disk
- Caching of objects in memory or on disk
- Minification of posts and pages and feeds
- Minification of inline, embedded, or 3rd party JavaScript (with automated updates)
- Minification of inline, embedded, or 3rd party CSS (with automated updates)

- Browser caching using cache-control, future expire headers, and entity tags (ETag) with "cache-busting "
- JavaScript grouping by template (home page, post page, etc.) with embed location control
- Non-blocking JavaScript embedding
- Importing of post attachments directly into Media Library (and CDN)

W3 Total Cache Plugin Installation

To install the **W3 Total Cache** plugin, go to the plugins management menu and select *"Add New."* In the search box that will then appear, type the full name of the plugin, which is *"W3 Total Cache"* and then press the [Search Plugins] button *(Figure 9-7)*.

FIGURE 9-7

In the list of plugins, look for the specific plugin you requested (usually listed on the very top). When you find it, press the *"Install Now"* link under the plugin's name *(Figure 9-8)*.

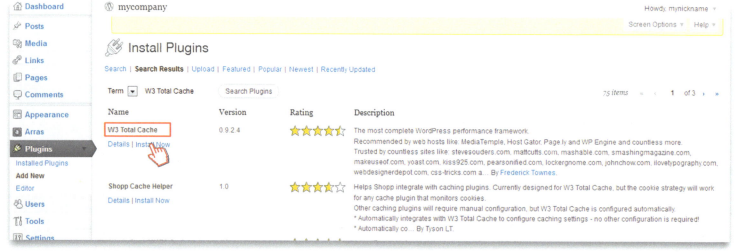

FIGURE 9-8

A pop-up window then appears, asking you, "Are you sure you want to install this plugin?" Just press the [OK] button to continue *(Figure 9-9)*.

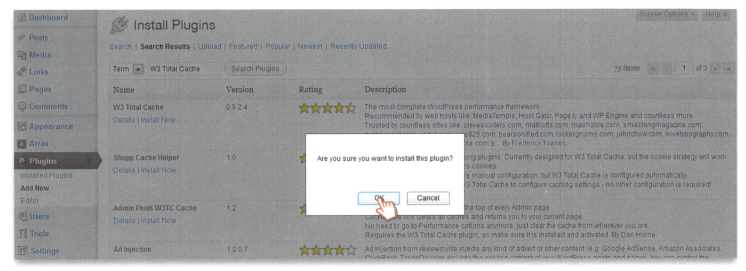

FIGURE 9-9

On the next screen the plugin informs you that the operation is complete, and you must press the *"Activate Plugin"* link to make the plugin work *(Figure 9-10)*.

FIGURE 9-10

A new option is available on the dashboard, under the settings menu, called *"Performance."* Click on it to make the necessary adjustments *(Figure 9-11)*.

FIGURE 9-11

W3 Total Cache Plugin Setup

In this section, I will show you how to configure basic settings on W3 Total Cache plugin. These settings are typically required in order to achieve the optimal functioning configuration. This configuration serves most website needs and will make your website load faster. First of all you must add caching rules to .htaccess file just by pressing the "auto-install" button.

Preview Mode

This option allows you to test the functionality of any change you make on W3 Total Cache plugin, before you apply these changes to your website. Leave this option disabled.

Page Cache

This option must be enabled, so as to allow all static pages to be cached. The latest version of each page will be cached in your web server's hard disk. So when a visitor of your website tries to access one of your static pages, this page will be loaded directly from the web server's disk.

Minify Static Script Files

Minification is the practice of removing unnecessary characters from code. It also combines and compresses

JS and CSS files, thus resulting to the reduction of their size. This process leads to decreased page load time. Enable this option and set *"Minify mode"* to Auto.

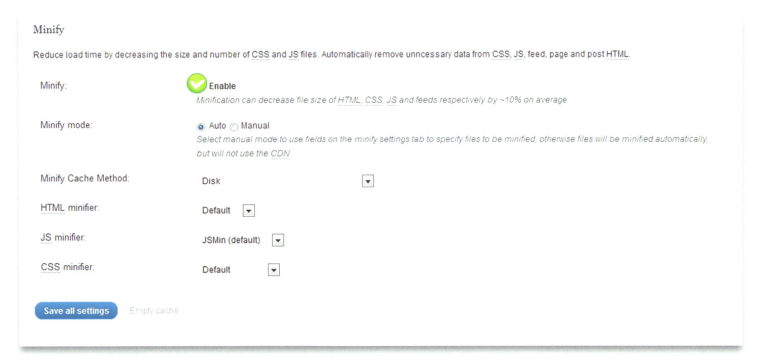

Database Cache

The database is a very delicate part of your WordPress website. So, only advanced users are allowed to experiment with it. I suggest that you leave this option disabled, in order to avoid any unwanted database errors that you don't know how to handle. In fact Database Cache feature helps caching database queries. So when a database query is made, it goes through the cache to speed up the process. This kind of caching is needed when a website has a high amount of traffic. Enable this feature when your website reaches more than 5000 visitors per day and if every post has more than 30 comments or replies.

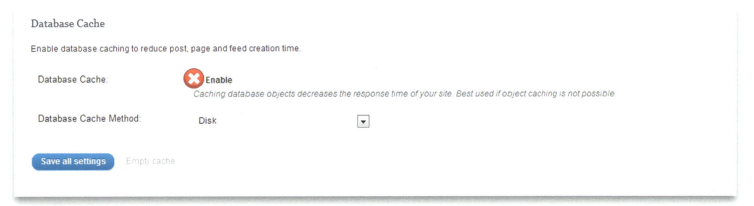

Object Cache

If you have already left Database Cache disabled, you must do so with Object Cache, because these features must function in correlation. Given the fact that your website is hosted on a shared server environment, you should consider disabling this option. This is because the disk usually responds slower than the database, in such an environment. On the other hand, if your website is hosted on a dedicated server environment, which means that you own the entire hard disk, then the database can work as fast as the hard drive, without any problems, so enabling Database Cache and Object Cache can considerably speed up the site.

Browser Cache

When a visitor accesses your website for the first time, the static files, such as images, css and JavaScript files are downloaded to the browser and stored in the browser's cache locally. The next time that the visitor will access your website, all these static files will be accessed from the cache. The Browser Cache feature of W3 Total Cache plugin helps in the setting of the behaviors of these cache-able files. It enables http compressions and specifies the expiration header for the files. The setting in browser cache helps the web browser to understand how to behave with the cache-able files. Enabling this option will increase the Page Load Speed.

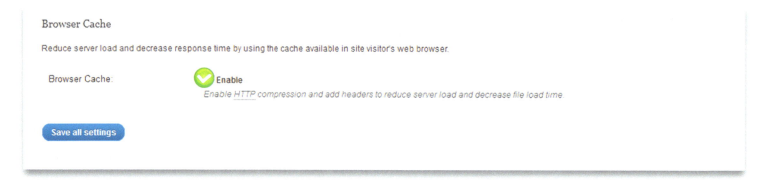

CDN (Content Delivery Network)

Leave this option disabled. W3 Total Cache provides you with some pre-configured, paid CDN providers. However, later in this book I will show you in details how to enable CDN on your website without any cost using Google App Engine.

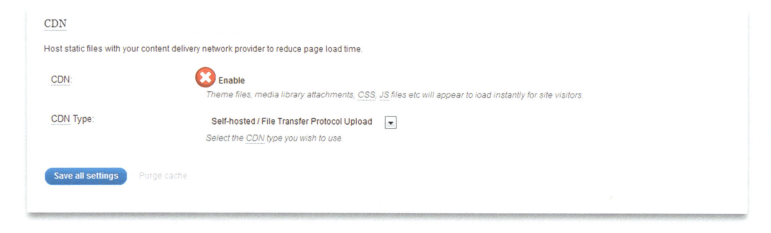

Network Performance & Security Powered by CloudFlare

Network Performance & Security powered by CloudFlare

CloudFlare protects and accelerates websites. Sign up now for free to get started, or if you have an account simply log in to obtain your API key from the account page to enter it below. Contact the CloudFlare support team with any questions.

CloudFlare: ☐ Enable

CloudFlare account email: admin

API key: ●●●●●● (find it here)

Domain:

Security level: High ▾

Development mode: Off ▾

Save all settings   Purge cache

CloudFlare is a free service that protects and accelerates any website online. Once a website is a part of the CloudFlare network, its web traffic is routed through CloudFlare's intelligent global network. This way the delivery of web pages is automatically optimized and the visitors get the fastest page load times, possible. It also blocks threats and limits abusive bots and crawlers, from wasting bandwidth and  server resources. CloudFlare websites experience significant improvement in performance and decrease in spam and other attacks. In fact CloudFlare acts as a cache proxy. When a visitor requests access to your website, CloudFlare first checks if the resource is in the local cache. CloudFlare caches parts of your website as static. For example, it caches things like images, CSS, and Javascript. Typically 60% of the resources on any given web page are cachable. What's great about that is, that if they have a local copy of your file, then they can deliver it directly to the visitor from a local data center and there for the load speed is extremely faster. On the other hand if they don't have a current copy in CloudFlare's cache, then they make a request from the data center back to your web server.

The main benefits for your website are:

- ◼ it loads twice as fast
- ◼ it uses 60% less bandwidth
- ◼ it has 65% fewer requests
- ◼ it is more secure from any kind of attacks.

To use CloudFlare you must first register at http://www.cloudflare.com, by clicking on the **Sign up now!** button and then follow the setup wizard. At the end of the process, you will be asked to change your domain's DNS server settings (*see page 3 ,"Connecting Domain name with Web Server"*), so that they point to the CloudFlare's

DNS servers. If your web server is hosted at Hostgator, the process is much simpler. Hostgator is a CloudFlare partner and therefore has made the setup process much easier, by adding a CloudFlare button on its cPanel *(Figure 9-12)*. Just select your domain name and activate the service. In a few minutes time, you will receive an email from Hostgator informing your that the process is complete and that from now on your website is a part of CloudFlare Network. This way, you don't need to change any DNS settings by hand. All the necessary adjustments have already been made for you, automatically by Hostgator.

FIGURE 9-12

Now that your website has become a part of CloudFlare Network, you must login to your CloudFlare account and access the account settings. Copy your account API key *(Figure 9-13)* and paste it to W3 Total Cache plugin CloudFlare settings section. Also fill in your domain name and set security level to medium. Finally enable the service and press the **Save all settings** button *(Figure 9-14)*.

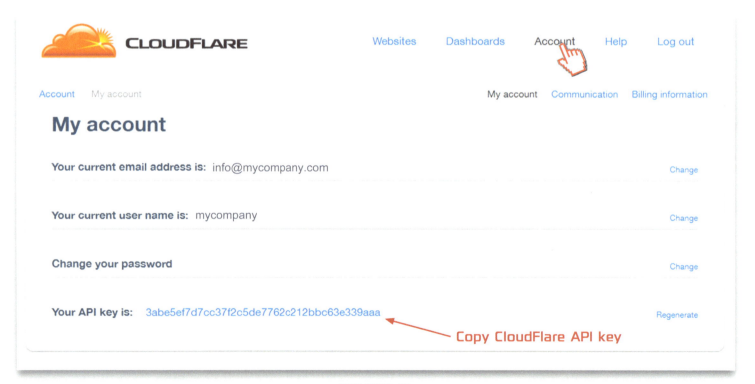

FIGURE 9-13

FIGURE 9-14

Miscellaneous

Disable *"Verify rewrite rules"* to avoid any future error messages regarding page cache. Disable *"File Locking"* if you are on shared hosting environments that use NFS, like the one I suggested earlier (*see page 2, "Linux-Based Hosting Plan"*). Enable *"Optimize disk enhanced page and minify caching for NFS",* to speed up caching. Most Linux based web servers support that feature. Disable *"News dashboard widget",* in order to have a nice and neat dashboard. Enable *"Google Page Speed dashboard widget",* to track your page load speed at any time. If you do enable this option, you must get a proper API key from Google.

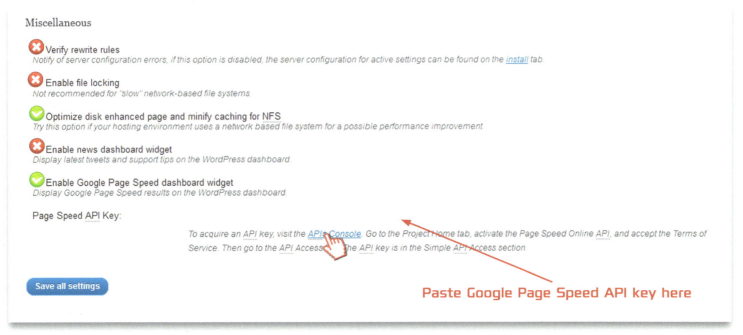

FIGURE 9-15

To get a Google Page Speed API key, you need to visit the **Google's APIs Console** at https://code.google.com/apis/console/, where you will login with your credentials to Create Project *(Figure 9-16)*. Then select *"Services"* from the menu and in the following list look for a service called **Page Speed Online API** *(Figure 9-17)*. Turn the service on *(Figure 9-18)*. Remember that the service has a limit of 250 queries per day. This means that if you access the dashboard more than 250 times a day, you will not get any page speed measurement data. Finally select API Access from the menu and copy the API key *(Figure 9-19)* and then paste it in the miscellaneous section of W3 Total Cache plugin *(Figure 9-15)*. Save all settings. Now you can access the dashboard and check your page speed score at any time *(Figure 9-20)*.

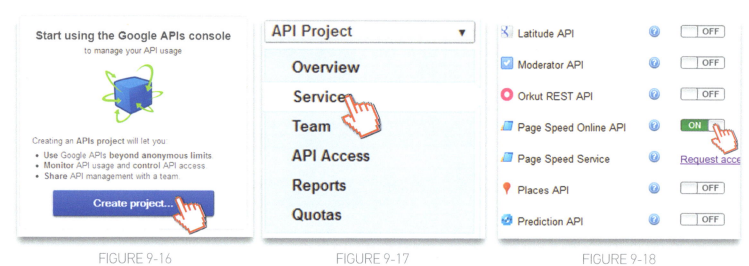

FIGURE 9-16   FIGURE 9-17   FIGURE 9-18

FIGURE 9-19

FIGURE 9-20

Measuring and Observing the Page Load Speed Time

Now that you are done tuning up your WordPress website, by disabling hot linking to images, enabling the caching mechanism and activating the CloudFlare services, it is time to measure and observe your website's load speed time, either in real time by using the YSlow Firefox add-on or from the Google Webmaster tools page speed measurement chart *(Figure 9-21)*. Always remember that Google's page speed measurement chart assesses the performance of your website in long term. So when you make an adjustment to you website, in order to improve its page load speed, Google will display the results when the crawler passes by your website. The rate with which Google crawler passes by your website, depends on how often you post new content.

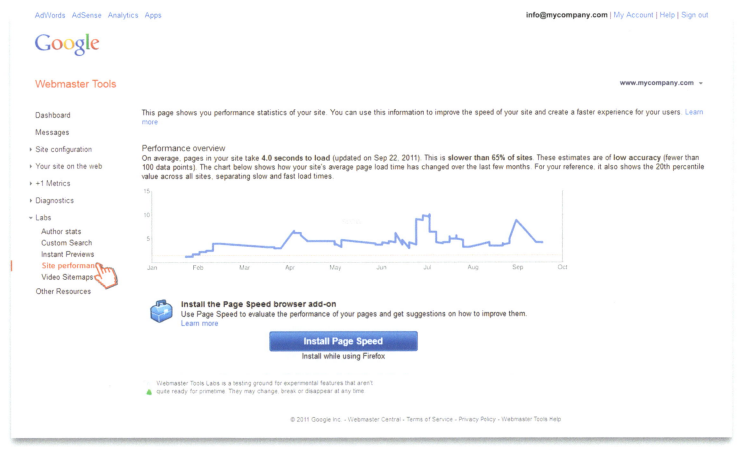

FIGURE 9-21

If the result of YSlow and Google Webmaster tools speed chart shows that your website is still slow, then you can optimize the page load speed time of your website even more, by also applying other optimization methods, such as **Content Delivery Network** and **Smush.it** as explained in the following Chapter.

Lightspeed WordPress With the Use of CDN

A content delivery network is a network of servers, spread all around the world. These servers contain copies of a website's content. By using a content delivery network, you can accelerate the load speed time up to 80%. The world's most popular websites use CDN to achieve better and faster performance.

How a Content Delivery Network (CDN) Works

When a Webmaster creates a dynamic website, he or she has to deal with two kinds of elements: the static ones, such as theme files, CSS files, Java files, Logo images; and the dynamic ones, which are images and videos contained in articles. During the development process, all files are hosted on the web server that you already own. When a visitor loads your website, all this content is transferred from your server to your visitor's device. With the use of CDN, however, all static and dynamic elements are not transferred by only one server to the visitor's device, but from several ones, at the same time. This way the user does not transfer all the content from just one server, exceeding of its bandwidth limit. However, the main advantage of using CDN is not the bandwidth management, but the acceleration of the load speed time. This is achieved thanks to the browser's ability to provide 8 simultaneous HTTP connections that all browsers can manage. Since all browsers can handle 8 different connections at the same time, why bother using only one server to distribute your content?

Technically, what the CDN does is to distribute your website's content to several servers, so when a user is loading your website, the content is transferred from these different servers to his or her device. This procedure as a whole results in lower bandwidth usage per connection, thus leading to faster page load speed. W3 Total Cache plugin, referred to earlier in this chapter, offers CDN as an embedded feature.

How to Use Content Delivery Network

A content delivery network is in fact a different type of hosting provider. Several well-established providers, such as Amazon, offer these kinds of services, charging per GB of transfer or per HTTP request. In order to connect the content of your website with a CDN provider, you don't need to be an expert—all you need to do is to install the W3 Cache plugin, which has an embedded CDN support service that does this for you. What a CDN Provider actually does is that it creates a mirror of the content of your website to its servers. If you want to know more about the charges and services provided, visit the two most popular CDN providers on the web, Amazon Cloud Front and MaxCDN. You can also try Speedy Mirror, which provides CDN services free of charge up to a specific limit, which is quite enough for you to try it out.

The goal of this book is to show you how to create an SEO website, without spending any money on buying services, so I suggest that you use Google App Engine as a CDN Provider. Google App Engine is a free-of-charge service that is provided to all developers as a platform of development, testing, and distribution of applications. You can also easily use Google App Engine as a CDN Provider. Just consider being able to take advantage of Google's servers and above all, free of charge.

Google App Engine as a CDN Provider

By using a CDN provider, the content of your website is allocated to various servers, without your personal interference. So when a user is visiting your website, this content is being transferred to the user by several servers and not just by yours, achieving faster load speed time, thanks to the simultaneous connections that the browser is able to support. CDN providers use different ways of dividing and sharing the content among these different servers, automatically and without any interference on behalf of the website's administrator. So, on the one hand, you can make your life a little bit easier, as everything is dealt with automatically; but on the other hand, you lose control of the website's content distribution, because its management is given in a way to the CDN provider. But what if the administrator wants to maintain full control of the content found in the CDN server distribution, at all times? The answer to this problem is found in the use of **Google App Engine** as a CDN provider. In fact, instead of indicating which files will be hosted to the CDN, as is the usual practice, you actually send the static files of your website to the CDN server (Google App Engine) yourself, following a simple procedure. This way you get to choose which files will be hosted by the CDN at all times.

Google App Engine is a cloud computing technology for developing and hosting web applications. It virtualizes applications across multiple servers and data centers. This service is given free of charge. Google is charging for this service only if the bandwidth consumed by the visitors of your website exceeds a specific limit. If you need more bandwidth, the charge is quite reasonable, about $0.12 /GB. If your website gets up to 10,000 visits per day, you will never have to pay for this service. Google App Engine can host static files, such as CSS files, Javascript files, and image files. These types of files do not change very often, so I advise you to host them on the Google server rather than your own, thereby achieving better load speed time, as the content is transferred to the visitor by the server that is nearer to him or her.

Setting Up Google App Engine as a CDN Provider

In order to use Google App Engine as a CDN provider, your need to sign up for an App Engine account. First *"Sign in"* to Google with your credentials at http://code.google.com/appengine and then click on the *"Sign up"* link *(Figure 10-1)*. You will be asked to re-type your password, to create your account.

FIGURE 10-1

Then click on the Create Application button to continue the account creation process *(Figure 10-2)*.

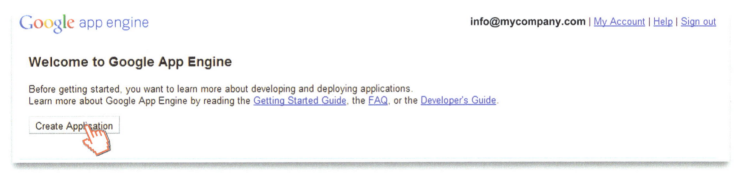

FIGURE 10-2

On the next screen fill in you mobile phone number to receive the verification code *(Figure 10-3)*.

FIGURE 10-3

After a few minutes you will receive an sms message from Google App Engine with the verification code. Fill in the code to complete the verification process *(Figure 10-4)*.

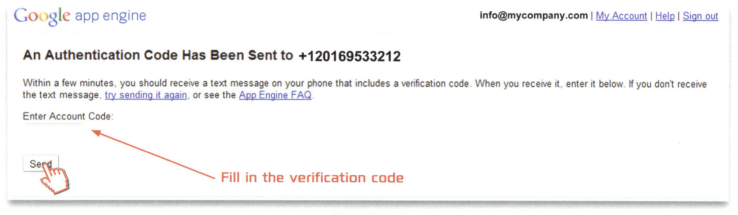

FIGURE 10-4

Type in an Application Identifier of your choice and press the Check Availability button. Also type in an Application Title. Leave all other options as is. Just check *"I accept the terms"* and click on the Create Application button to finish *(Figure 10-5)*.

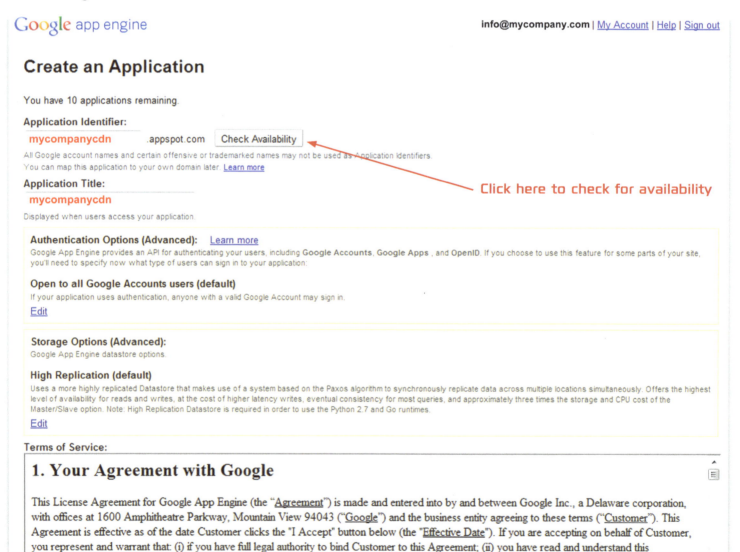

FIGURE 10-5

You now have an active Google App Engine account and a subdomain (mycompany.appspot.com) that is hosted on Google and ready to host any static files you choose *(Figure 10-6)*. In the next paragraph, I will explain to you in details how to upload these files to your new CDN server.

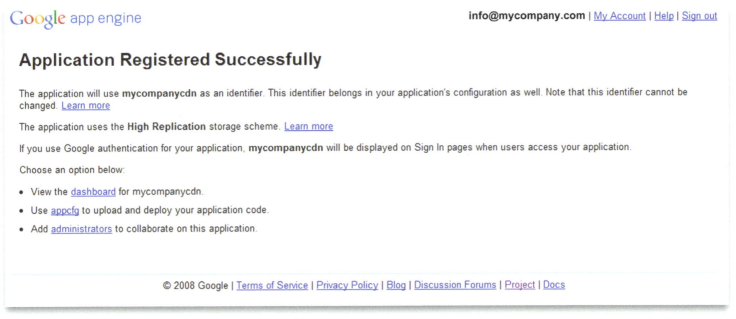

FIGURE 10-6

Uploading Files to Google App Engine

Now it's time to upload some of your files to Google App Engine. Go to the homepage of Google App Engine and on the *"Getting Started"* section click the link on the second step that says *"Download the App Engine SDK"* *(Figure 10-7)* or go to the following URL http://code.google.com/appengine/downloads.html to download the **App Engine SDK application**.

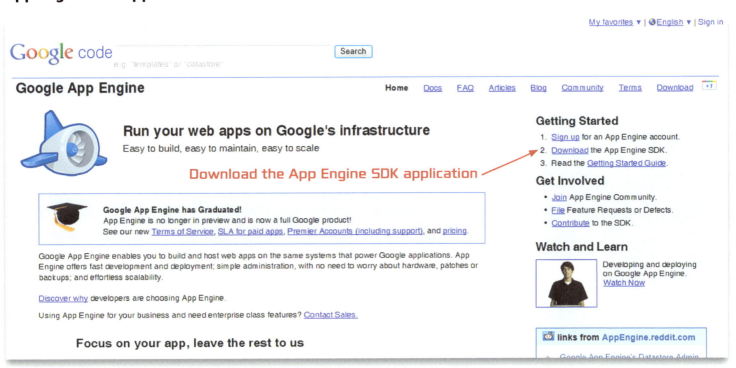

FIGURE 10-7

Download the Google App Engine SDK application for Python. Select the application package that suits your platform. In the following example I'm using the package for Microsoft Windows.

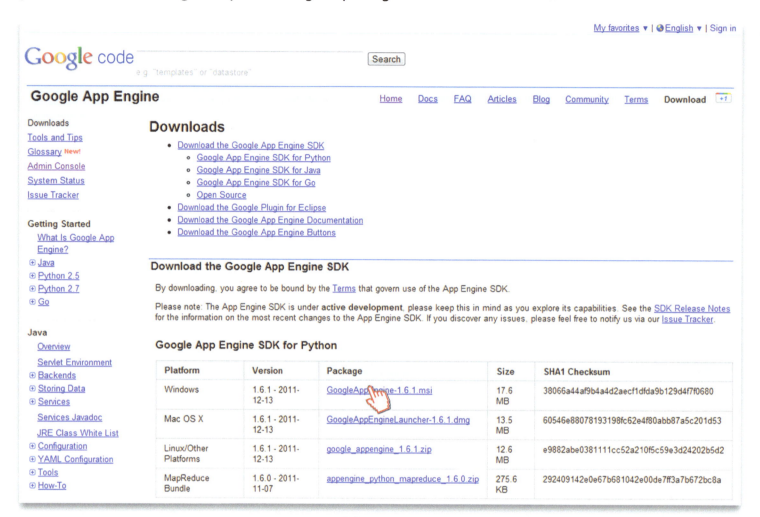

FIGURE 10-8

FIGURE 10-9

Run the Google App Engine SDK application installer that you have downloaded earlier. On the first screen of the installer press the **ActiveState Python** button *(Figure 10-9)* to download the **Python** package which is absolutely necessary for the Google App Engine SDK application to work *(Figure 10-10)*. Alternatively you can download ActiveState Python by following the link http://www.activestate.com/activepython/downloads/. Do not close the Google App Engine SDK application installer. You will continue after you're done with the ActiveState Python installation.

FIGURE 10-10

When you are done installing ActiveState Python *(Figure 10-11)*, continue with the installation process of the Google App Engine SDK application by pressing the `Next` button *(Figure 10-12)*.

FIGURE 10-11

FIGURE 10-12

Now that you have successfully installed Google App Engine SDK, a new icon appears on your desktop, called *Google App Engine Launcher*.

Start the **Google App Engine Launcher**, go to *"edit"* and then *"preferences"* to configure the application *(Figure 10-13)*. At the *"Python Path"* field, press the [Select...] button and locate the python executable on your local hard disk, which is usually located at *"C:\Python27\python.exe"*. At the *"App Engine SDK"* field, press the [Select...] button and locate the installation folder of App Engine, which is usually located at "C:\Program Files (x86)\Google\google_appengine". At the "Editor" field, press the [Select...] button and locate a text editor like MS Windows Notepad, which is usually located at *"C:\Windows\ notepad.exe"*. Leave the *"Development Server"* field empty *(Figure 10-14)*.

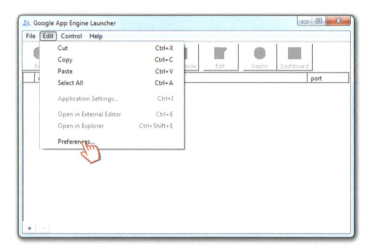

FIGURE 10-13

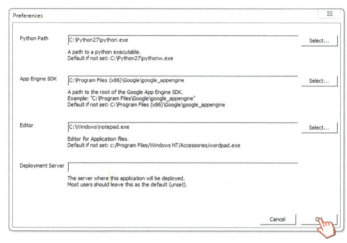

FIGURE 10-14

Next, on the Google App Engine Launcher, select *"File"* and then *"Create New Application" (Figure 10-15)*. In the *"Application Name"* field *(Figure 10-16)* type the application identifier that you have already chosen when you registered your application to Google App Engine *(Figure 10-5)*. At the *"Parent Directory"* field, press the [Browse...] button and select a folder. In this folder all application configuration files will be saved. Also, this is the folder where you will put all your .jpg .css .js CDN files. So select a location that is within easy reach (e.g. on your desktop). Finally press the [Create] button to finish the setup of your very first application.

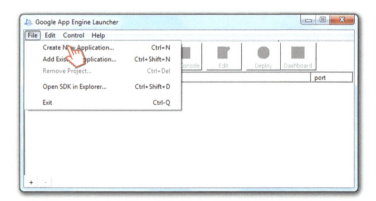

FIGURE 10-15

FIGURE 10-16

Check the folder that you selected previously *(Figure 10-16)* and you will see a new folder that has been created inside it, called *"mycompanycdn"*. In the folder *"mycompanycdn"*, create a sub-folder for every file family you want to upload to CDN. For example, I have created a sub-folder for all image files, called *"images"* and one for all stylesheet files, called *"styles" (Figure 10-17)*.

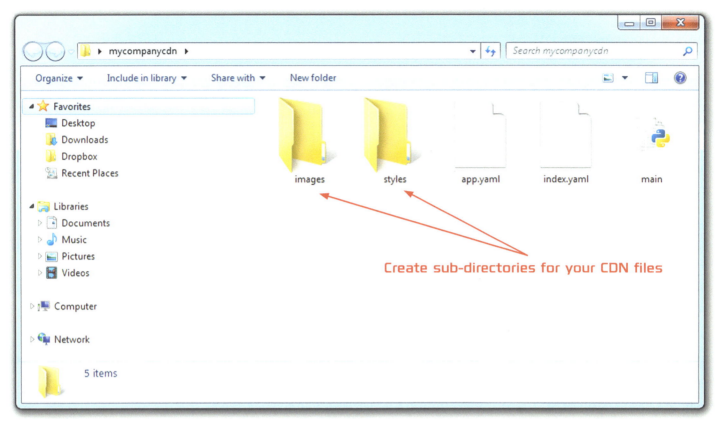

FIGURE 10-17

Place a couple of image files inside the *"images"* sub-folder that you have created. These image files will be uploaded later to the Google App Engine, as a part of your newly established Content Delivery Network. Go back to Google App Engine application and notice that on the main window now appears the *"mycompanycdn"* application, that you have previously created. Select it and then press the ✎ button on the toolbar *(Figure 10-18)*.

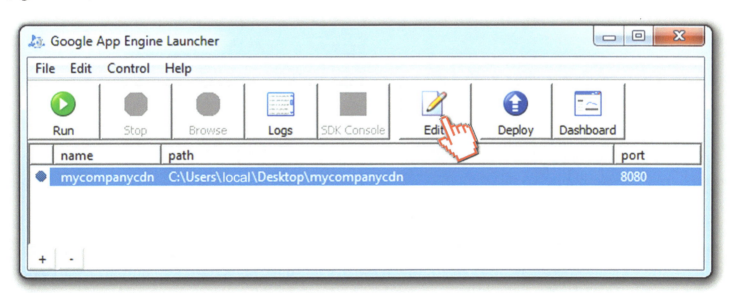

FIGURE 10-18

Once you press the ✎ button, Windows Notepad will appear and the app.yaml file, which is in fact your CDN's configuration file, will be ready to be edited *(Figure 10-19)*.

```
app.yaml - Notepad                                          ☐ ⊡ ✕

File  Edit  Format  View  Help
application: mycompanycdn
version: 1
runtime: python
api_version: 1

handlers:
- url: /favicon\.ico
  static_files: favicon.ico
  upload: favicon\.ico

- url: .*
  script: main.py |
```

FIGURE 10-19

The *"app.yaml"* configuration file must contain your application identifier and the version number. You must also declare the sub-directories' structure that you will use in order to place your CDN files. So type your application identifier in the first line of *"app.yaml"* configuration file at the *"application:"* field. Leave the *"version"*, *"runtime"* and *"api_version"* fields as is. Go to the 6th line and delete everything below *"handlers: "*. Here you must type the sub-directories' names that you created earlier *(Figure 10-17)*. So when you put it all together the final CDN version of app.yaml configuration file will look like this *(Figure 10-20)*.

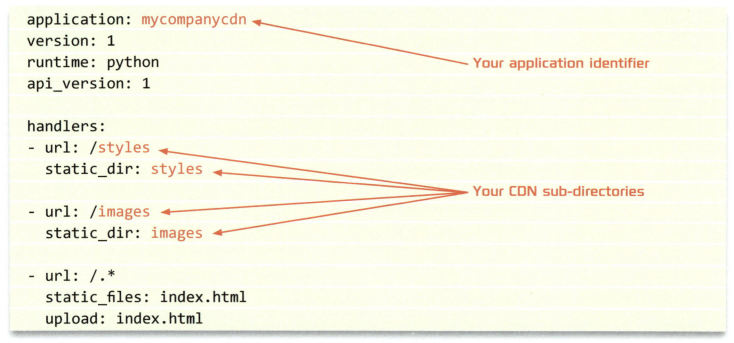

```
application: mycompanycdn ◄─────────────┐
version: 1
runtime: python                          ├── Your application identifier
api_version: 1


handlers:
- url: /styles ◄─────────────┐
  static_dir: styles ◄────┐  │
                          ├──┴── Your CDN sub-directories
- url: /images ◄──────────┘
  static_dir: images ◄────┘


- url: /.*
  static_files: index.html
  upload: index.html
```

FIGURE 10-20

When you are done editing the *"app.yaml"* configuration file, just save all changes made. Your next move is to upload the *"styles"* and *"images"* sub-directories, including the ones contained in Google servers under your Google App Engine Application sub-domain. To achieve that you must press the [Deploy] button on the Google App Engine Launcher toolbar. A new window will pop-up asking you to fill in your Google App Engine credentials *(Figure 10-21)*. Type your email and password and then press the [OK] button.

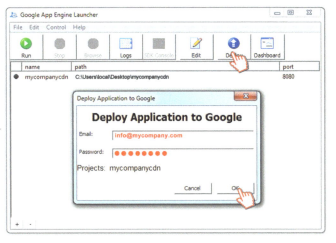

FIGURE 10-21

Then the Google App Engine Launcher will connect to your Google account. So by following the *"app.yaml"* configuration file, the Google App Engine Launcher will create the *"mycompanycnd"* application. In the *"mycompanycnd"* application, the Google App Engine Launcher will create the two CDN sub-directories *"Styles"* and *"Images."* After the creation of the two folders, it will also transfer to the *"mycompanycnd"* application, the content of these folders regardless of the type of the files.

FIGURE 10-22

You can study the whole process at the log window that opens when you press the deploy button *(Figure 10-22)*. Check if the deployment of the files was successful on the log window. If the log shows that the deployment was successful, then the uploading process has finished. After you have succeeded in the uploading process, it is time to put your Google CDN server on the test. Type in your favorite browser the name of the application identifier (mycompanycdn), followed by the domain of Google App Engine(.appspot.com). Add a slash (/) and then the sub-directory's name (images),- slash (/) the file name you want to access (dog_cdn.jpg).

The CDN link will look like this *(Figure 10-23)*:

http://mycompanycdn.appspot.com/images/dog_ cdn.jpg

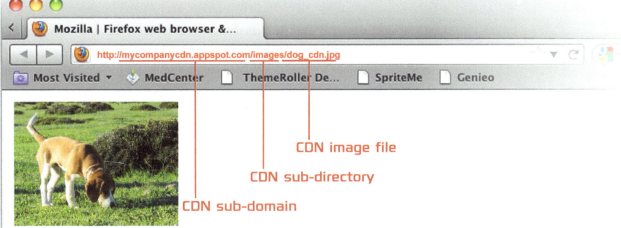

FIGURE 10-23

From now on when you want to upload some files to your Google CDN server, just add them in these two folders and then press the 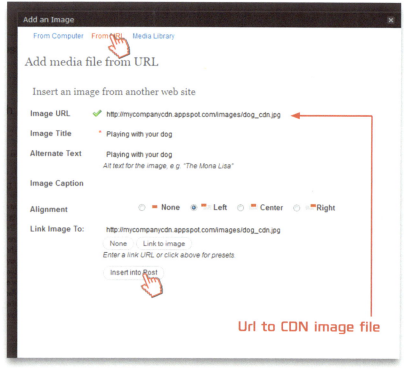 button on the Google App Engine Launcher toolbar. And what if only two folders are not enough and you need some more? Then the only thing you need to do, is to create more sub-directories inside the "mycompanycdn" directory locally and add the sub-directories' names in the app.yaml configuration file, by pressing Edit on the App Engine Launcher toolbar and then deploy them to your Google CDN server.

Connecting WordPress With Google App Engine CDN Files

There are many, alternative ways on how to connect WordPress with the files that are hosted in Google App Engine CDN and it is up to you to decide on which one you choose based on you level of expertise and on the amount of files you want to spread between your hosting server and the Google CDN server.

Adding images to posts or pages from CDN server

In Chapter 3 (*see page 24, "Adding Images"*) your have already learned how to add images to posts or pages from your local hard disk. When you add an image to WordPress, the image is uploaded to your web server in a specific sub-folder of WordPress. Now that you have a CDN server in your disposal, remember, when you create a new post or page, that you must first upload the images that you are going to use, to the CDN server and then insert them in posts or pages of your website. This way the images will be loaded from the CDN server and not from your own web server. You can add images, hosted on the CDN server, to new posts or to old ones, if you want to improve the page load time, site-wide. This will significantly speed up your page load time thanks to the simultaneous connection to different servers that all the modern browsers are able to handle.

So from now on, if you want your website to load faster, upload the images to the CDN server and then instead of pressing the *"From Computer"* tab on the *"Add an image"* pop-up window of WordPress, you must press the *"From URL"* tab. In the field *"Image URL"*, type the url of the image that you want to add to the post, which is hosted at your CDN server (Figure 10-24). Fill in all the other fields as usually and press the (Insert into Post) button. To verify that the image has been loaded from the CDN server on the post toolbar, press the HTML tab and notice the url of the image. If the url of the image starts with the Google App Engine sub-domain, then you have successfully loaded an image to your post from your CDN server (*Figure 10-25*).

FIGURE 10-24

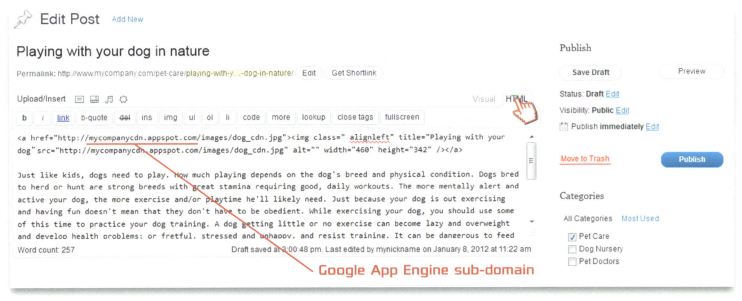

FIGURE 10-25

Hosting all Static images to the CDN server

To get even faster page load speed, you can follow the same procedure that I previously described, with all the images of your website, starting with the static ones. Static images are all the images that are not included in posts. Images like the logo of your website, social media buttons, banner ads and sidebar images are considered static images. So gather all the static images of your website and place them inside the local "images" CDN sub-directory *(Figure 10-17)*. Deploy them to your CDN server, using Google App Engine Launcher and then start replacing the existing images with the ones that are now hosted at the CDN server. Start by replacing the images that are easier to access, such as your website's logo, which is probably located at your theme's option page *(Figure 10-26)*, as well as your sidebar images, which are usually located at the WordPress widget area *(Figure 10-27)*.

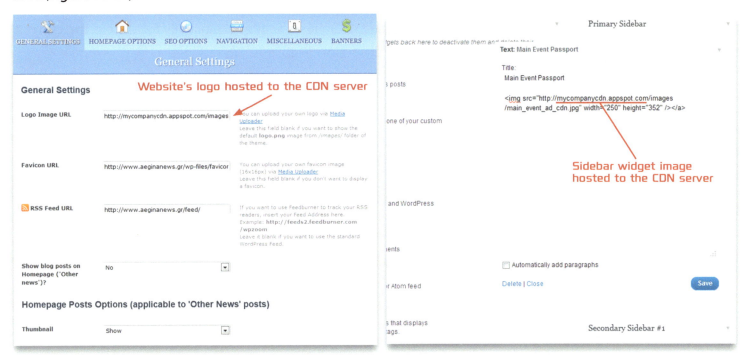

FIGURE 10-26   FIGURE 10-27

Apart from the images, WordPress has a lot of other static files. Files, such as stylesheets and javascripts, that are used either by the WordPress theme or by the installed plugins. You can also host these files at the CDN server, in order to get faster page load speed but because of the importance of these files, you must be extra careful when handling them. Stylesheets are responsible for the graphical look of WordPress and javascripts are responsible for the functionality of the plugins. So if a file is not connected to WordPress properly, it will result to a broken graphical theme or a disfunctional plugin. To have these files loaded from your CDN server, you must first upload the files to the CDN server and then change the links inside the WordPress theme or inside the plugins code. First download the files from the WordPress installation directory, using your favorite FTP client *(Figure 10-28)* and then upload them to the CDN server, using Google App Engine Launcher.

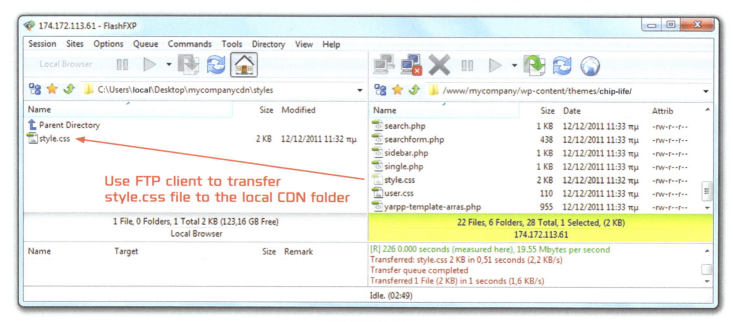

FIGURE 10-28

Finally replace **<?php bloginfo('stylesheet_url'); ?>** with the CDN's link to *style.css* file *(Figure 10-29)*. This file's link is not easy to locate by the novice WordPress user. Stylesheet files are usually located in the current theme's header.php file, between <head> and </head> section *(Figure 10-30)*.

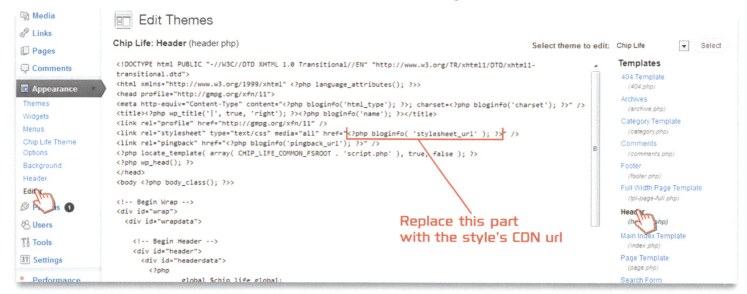

FIGURE 10-29

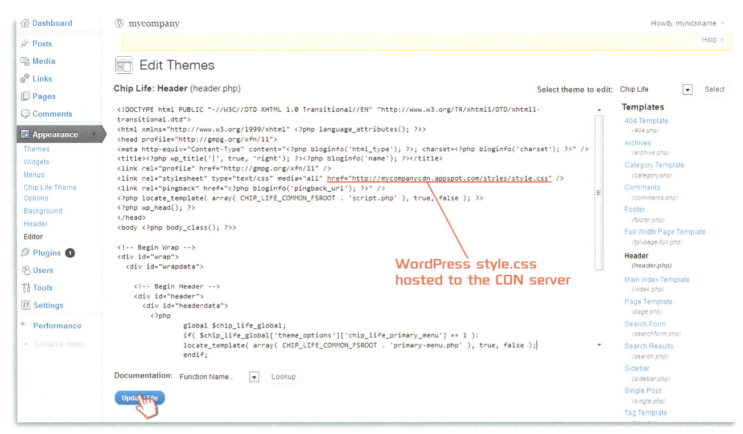

FIGURE 10-30

If you want to further increase the page load speed, do the same with other types of files, such as Javascripts and xml files. The more files your website loads from the CDN server, the faster the page load speed.

Reduce Image Size to Speed Up WordPress

One of the most important rules that all Webmasters must follow in order to achieve fast load speed time is to keep the images as small as possible. This of course should not mean that you sacrifice quality. Consider having on your homepage 5 to10 articles containing images with a size of more than 100 KB. Using any available image-processing application, such as Photoshop, Fireworks or GIMP, you could turn images of 100 KB into 20-KB ones. This way, just by changing the image size, the load speed time would improve by 80%. However, you can still improve the images' size by using the **WP Smush.it** plugin.

WP Smush.it Plugin

Yahoo developers have come up with a technique that enables you to decrease the image size without losing any quality. This technique is applied just by using the Smush.it plugin, with no effort required by the administrator. All you need to do is to install and activate the plugin. From then on, every time you insert one or more images to an article, the plugin takes over and strips the image of all unnecessary bytes, without altering it in any way in terms of quality, thus downsizing it. Always bear in mind that the smaller the volume of a website's parts, the faster its load speed time.

WP Smush.it Plugin Installation

To install the **WP Smush.it**, go to the plugins management menu and select *"Add New."* In the search box that will then appear, type the full name of the plugin, which is *"WP Smush.it"* and then press the Search Plugins button *(Figure 10-31).*

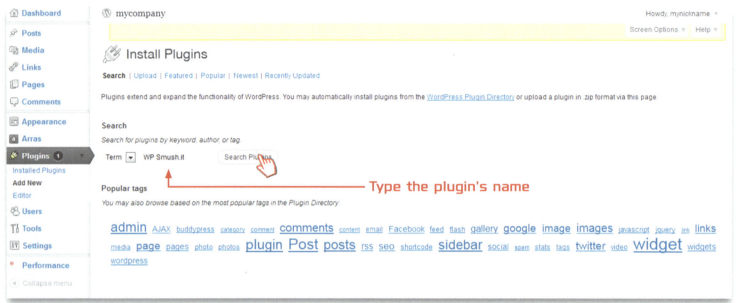

FIGURE 10-31

In the list of plugins, look for the specific plugin you requested (usually listed on the very top). When you find it, press the *"Install Now"* link under the plugin's name *(Figure 10-32).*

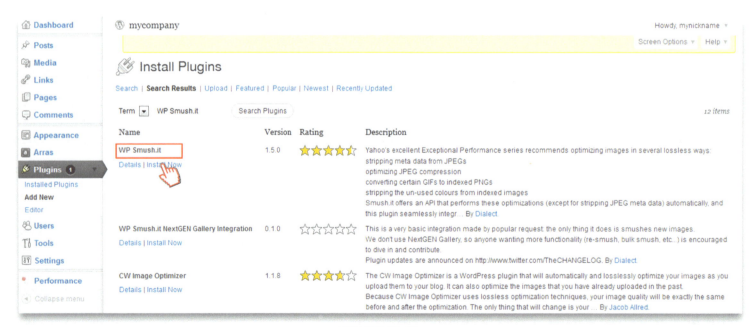

FIGURE 10-32

A pop-up window then appears, asking you, *"Are you sure you want to install this plugin?"* Just press the OK button to continue *(Figure 10-33).*

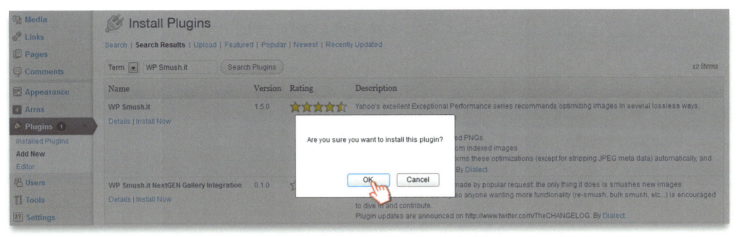

FIGURE 10-33

On the next screen the plugin informs you that the operation is complete, and you must press the *"Activate Plugin"* link to make the plugin work *(Figure 10-34)*.

FIGURE 10-34

From now on, when you upload an image to WordPress in order to attach it in an article, the image's size will be automatically optimized. Images that have been uploaded in the past, must be optimized manually from the WordPress Media Library, by pressing the *"smush.it now"* link *(Figure 10-35)*.

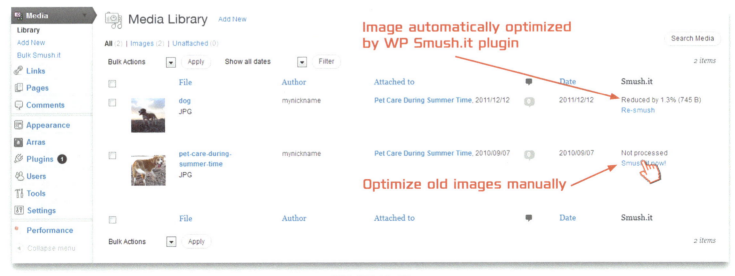

FIGURE 10-35

So Now I Have an SEO Website. What's Next?

You now are in possession of a website, which is not only Google friendly, but also built according to SEO rules. Furthermore, your website was not created by some expert, but by yourself, easily and in no time, based on guidelines that Google loves. But what if you want to promote your website even more and not just by using organic traffic, but through other sources as well? Another source that will give your website even more traffic is social media. Much is said on whether or not social media bring in benefits when used as a marketing tool. However it is an undisputable fact that social networks, such as Facebook and Twitter, have entered our everyday life, as they are being used by millions of users every day, mostly as a communication tool. In this chapter I will show you how your website can receive traffic through social media. This method refers to websites containing news articles, or corporate websites with products or services, residing in cities of 30,000 up to 50,000 people.

The Local Power of Facebook

Facebook is a social network service based on human relationships. Its users are related to one another through real or just online relationships. Via this network they publish text, images, and videos that they think is of interest to their friends. Using the power of publishing on Facebook, you can get more traffic. In this chapter, I will show you how to create a friend/customer base and how to publish the content of your website on Facebook automatically.

Facebook Profile VS Facebook Page or Group

Our suggestion is to create a new profile, destined to meet only the needs of your website. It is not advised to create a group within your personal profile because, as various researches indicate, most Facebook users avoid registering to groups, as they do not want to be spammed on a daily basis by annoying advertising campaigns. On the other hand, a page has limited potentiality and cannot properly serve your launching needs. So firstly you need to create a Facebook profile for your website. The name of the profile should be a combination of the words contained in your domain name. For example, if your domain name is essexpetshop.com, your profile's first name could be Essex and its last name Petshop or Essexpetshop and

.com accordingly. Try several different combinations until Facebook finally accepts your name. Once your account is created, add your website's logo as your personal profile picture. Then, send a friend request to your personal profile. Log in to Facebook with your personal profile and accept the friend request submitted by your company profile. So far you have created a Facebook profile for your company which has only one friend. The next step is to create a huge friend list for this profile, as fast as possible. The usual way to "make" friends is to send friend requests to all the people suggested to you by Facebook, whether you know them or not. At first this technique will actually work well for you, because your profile has no friends at all and such an action is allowed by Facebook. But when you reach the level of 100 or more friends, massive friend requests are considered spamming, action that is punished by Facebook with a 48-hour blockage of the friend request ability. If you continue this practice, the blockage is increased to 7 days and so on, climbing up to several months.

The answer to this problem is Facebook's mechanism called friend suggestion. Instead of sending friend requests, you have other friends of yours suggesting you to their own. This technique is not subject to any limitation or punishment. The only restriction is that one can make 50 friend suggestions at a time. This way you can ask all your closest friends to recommend you to their friends. You should first ask the ones with the higher number of friends, so you can form a list of friends/potential customers quickly, easily, and without the fear of a possible Facebook exclusion.

Post Content From WordPress to Facebook Automatically

The goal now is to publish every article of your website on your Facebook profile, automatically. To achieve this, you will need to use a free of charge service called **dlvr.it**. The dlvr.it website takes over the publication of your website's content on Facebook, Twitter, and Linked in, using the RSS feed of your site. There are of course other websites providing the same service as well, but I suggest that you use dlvr.it because it is quite reliable and mostly because when it takes your article via the RSS feed, it also attaches to it the first image it finds in the article. This way, your website's article is posted on your Facebook profile complete with its title, its image, and its text as opposed to what other similar services do (they post only title and text). The procedure is quite simple. Just go to http://dlvr.it/ and create an account. By using the power of dlvr.it you will achieve the automatic publication of every new article to all your Facebook friends.

Using dlvr.it to Distribute Your Website's Content to Facebook

If you want to use dlvr.it to distribute your website's content to Facebook, go to http://dlvr.it, fill in your email and a password and then press the sign up button *(Figure 11-1)*. On the next screen, fill in your domain name and then add a trailing slash and the word *"feed"* (http://www.mycompany.com/feed). This is the link to your website's RSS feed. You must also select the option *"Post all items existing in feed now"* and press the next button *(Figure 11-2)*. Then choose your destination, which in this case is Facebook, and press the *"f"* button *(Figure 11-3)*. You will then be transferred to facebook and you will be asked to give permission to dlvr.it to post content to your facebook account. Then, go back to the dlvr.it web brower tab and from the drop down menu, select where the content of your website will be posted. If you have created a Facebook profile for your website, then select the *"Personal Profile"* option *(Figure 11-4)*. Finally press the [Continue] button to complete the process and see your "New Route" to facebook *(Figure 11-5)*.

FIGURE 11-1

FIGURE 11-3

FIGURE 11-2

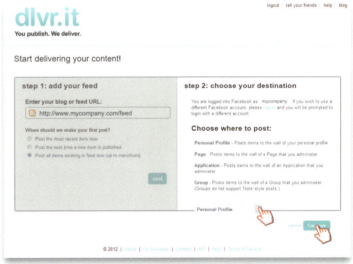

FIGURE 11-4

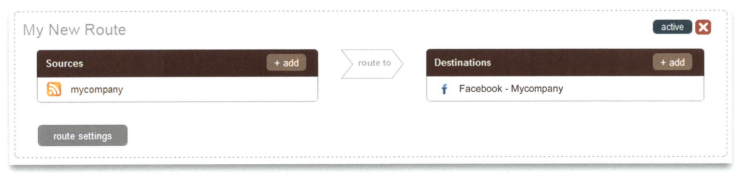

FIGURE 11-5

Facebook "Like" Is Sexier Than Link Sharing

As previously mentioned, by using the service dlvr.it, all of your articles will be posted on your Facebook profile; however, this has a limited number of members. But how amazing would it be if every reader of your article were able to post it on his or her own profile, so that all of that person's own friends would be able to read it as well? The new leader in link sharing is Facebook's *"Like,"* because it is sexier than link sharing. The average user is accustomed to pressing the *"Like"* button, which is easier than using the *"Share"* button simply because he or she does so on a daily basis to friends' pictures, comments, and videos. So when the Facebook user sees a *"Like"* button, he or she does not hesitate to use it. The moment a reader of your article presses *"Like,"* this article is automatically posted on his or her Facebook wall. This way your article is seen by all of your reader's friends. On average, every Facebook user has at least 130 friends. Even if only one visitor of your website presses *"Like"* for the article he or she is reading, then a potential visitor base is created by Facebook for your website. And all that is achieved just by one and only one visitor. Supposing that 10 visitors press *"Like,"* then over 1,300 people are automatically able to see the article hosted on your website. So the odds are that they will end up visiting your website, just by pressing the article's link on the Facebook. This service is provided by the use of the **Facebook Open Graph: I Like Button** plugin.

Facebook I Like Button Plugin Installation

To install the **Facebook I Like Button**, go to the plugins management menu and select *"Add New."* In the search box that will then appear, type the full name of the plugin, which is *"Facebook I Like Button"* and then press the [Search Plugins] button *(Figure 11-6)*.

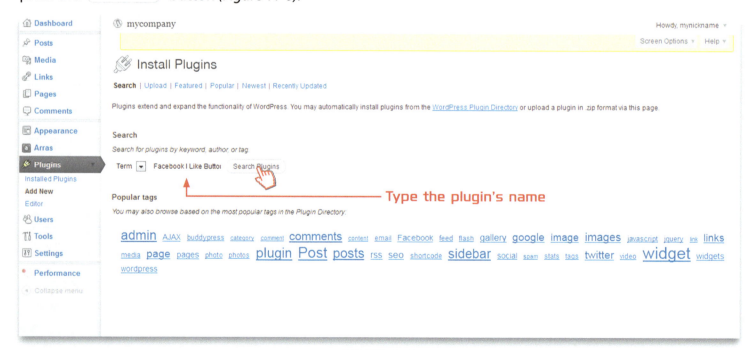

FIGURE 11-6

In the list of plugins, locate the *"Facebook I Like Button"* plugin by Radu Boncea and press the *"Install Now"* link under the plugin's name *(Figure 11-7)*.

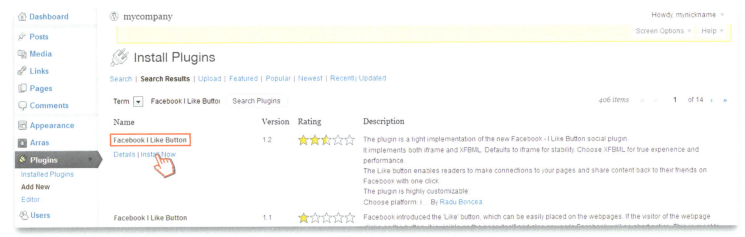

FIGURE 11-7

A pop-up window then appears, asking you, *"Are you sure you want to install this plugin?"*
Just press the [OK] button to continue *(Figure 11-8)*.

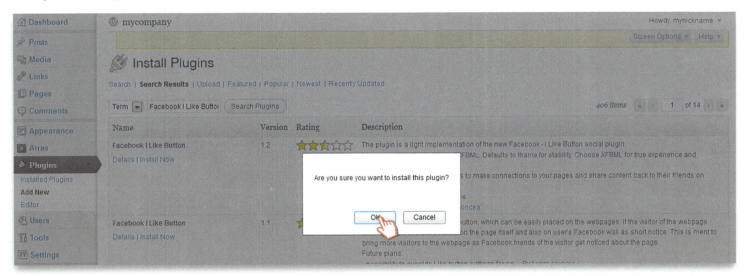

FIGURE 11-8

On the next screen the plugin informs you that the operation is complete, and you must press the *"Activate Plugin"* link to make the plugin work *(Figure 11-9)*.

FIGURE 11-9

Then select *"FB I Like Button"* in the WordPress settings panel, in order to make the necessary adjustments *(Figure 11-10)*.

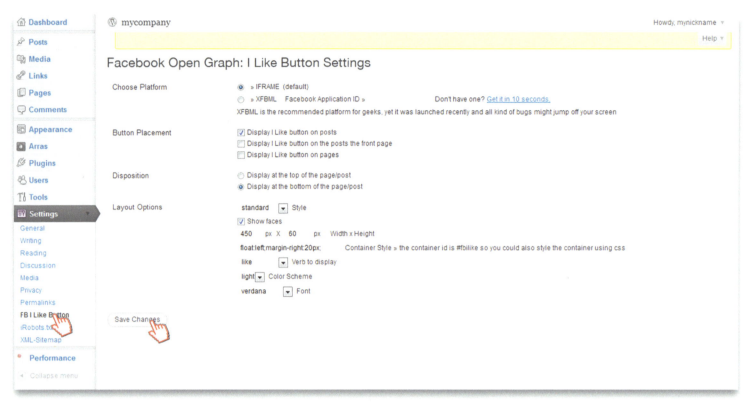

FIGURE 11-10

Google +1 Button: Google's Version of the "Like" Button

In the second half of the year 2011, a new button showed up on the Google search results page. This new button appeared right next to the titles of the results, enabling the user to show his or her preference to a website just by pressing it. This button is called +1 and works as a voting system. When the user presses the +1 button, the user's preference to the website is recorded and he or she is therefore giving the website a vote of appreciation. The +1 button is in fact similar to the commonly used Facebook *"Like"* button. And as we all know, the more *"Likes"* a post has, the more popular it is. But what is the actual purpose of the +1 button and where are these +1 preference manifestations registered and shown? In fact, the +1s are the recommendations of a visitor to all other potential visitors. What's important is that the +1s are registered and displayed on Google's Webmaster Tools. The fact that the +1s are stored and can be accessed on Google Webmaster Tools is the tangible proof of their importance, as every element included in Google Webmaster Tools can be a present or future SEO factor.

WordPress Google +1 Button Plugin Installation

To install the **WordPress Google +1 Button**, go to the plugins management menu and select *"Add New."* In the search box that will then appear, type the full name of the plugin, which is *"WordPress Google +1 Button"* and then press the ⸨ Search Plugins ⸩ button *(Figure 11-11)*.

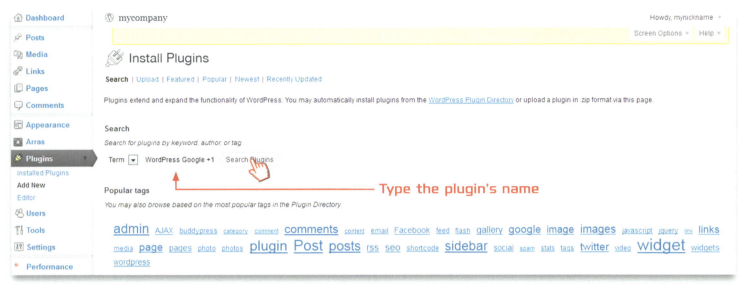

FIGURE 11-11

In the list of plugins, locate the "WordPress Google +1 Button" plugin by Jacob Gillespie and press the *"Install Now"* link under the plugin's name *(Figure 11-12)*.

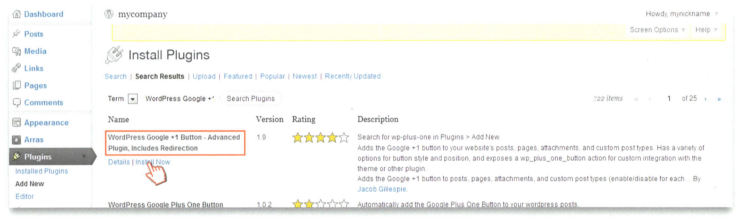

FIGURE 11-12

A pop-up window then appears, asking you, *"Are you sure you want to install this plugin?"* Just press the [OK] button to continue *(Figure 11-13)*.

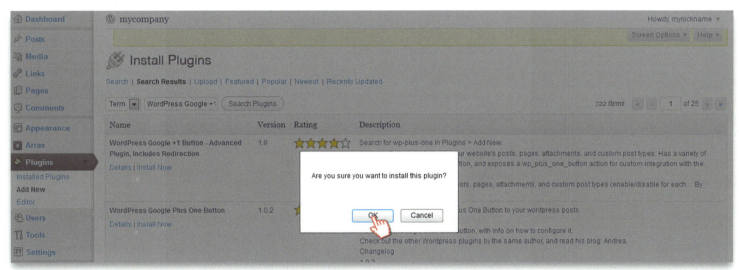

FIGURE 11-13

On the next screen the plugin informs you that the operation is complete, and you must press the *"Activate Plugin"* link to make the plugin work *(Figure 11-14)*.

FIGURE 11-14

Then select *"Google +1 Button"* in the WordPress settings panel, in order to make the necessary adjustments *(Figure 11-15)*.

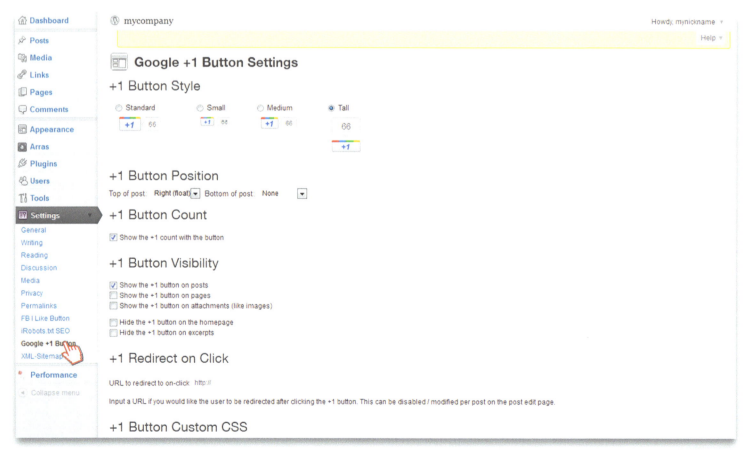

FIGURE 11-15

Inform the World About Your New Website Manually

Google may be the best way for someone to find your website, but it is not the only way. Even Google itself, during its first steps, did not rely on advertisement via the Internet in order to establish its reputation. Instead, it used as a promoting tool the previous experience of its visitors who put in a good word for its services. So Google has continued using the same method up to this day, through the link popularity technique that ranks the websites in the search results page. The main purpose is to let the world know about your new website, by any means. In this section, you will find the easiest and most effective ways of advertising that can be applied in most cases of websites targeting groups of people (cities) of up to 50,000 people.

Send Press Releases to all local newspapers and media.

Form a brief mailing list of the local newspapers, magazines, and news websites. Write a press release that gives a short description of what your website is about, and send it to the mailing list you have already formed. These local media will publish your press release eventually and your website will get immediate traffic once they do.

Stick your Logo stickers in public places.

Make small stickers, not bigger than 15 cm x 4 cm, with your URL or website logo, and stick them in places where people most frequently gather, such as bus and metro stations, pedestrian crossing pillars, and phone booths. You can also stick them on the back of your car or motorcycle and suggest that your friends do so as well. Personally, I always keep some stickers in my car and under my motorcycle's seat, so as to stick one in every crowded public place I visit, any chance I get. The cost of 100 such stickers will not exceed the amount of $20.

Make T-Shirts with your URL or logo.

One of the best ways to get people talking about your website is to give them free stuff. Since individuals love to receive things for no cost, they will surely start talking about your website. Make some T-shirts with your website's URL or logo and give them out to your friends and relatives. All these people will be your moving advertisements. Their cost will be below $50 in total.

Sign every post you make in blogs and forums with your URL.

Whenever you communicate online with the rest of the world, always include your website's URL in your signature. When you participate in online discussions, in forums, blogs, or social media, always include your URL as a signature.

Getting More SEO Information

You have successfully reached the end of the fascinating SEO journey. I hope that the instructions given in this book were explained in a simple and easy-to-apply way and that the screen shots helped you better understand the procedures you must follow. If you have followed word-by-word the guidelines provided in this book, you will see your website climbing up the stairs of Google's search results page. However, to enjoy the benefits of the SEO techniques to the highest degree, you must not stop at this point. You should always keep in touch with the latest news of SEO applications. Google evolves its methods constantly in order to provide more accurate information to its users. That is why all SEO marketing professionals, including the author, keep an eye on these innovations and try to understand how they work in order to apply them successfully to future and existing web marketing projects. You can easily track all these new innovations by following up on the resources available below . At these locations you can find all the latest news, techniques, and SEO methods through articles, online discussions, posts, and new editions of the present book that will be regularly posted and published.

Thank you for reading this book, and I hope you enjoyed reading it as much as I did writing it.

Website
Visit my website for helpful SEO Advices:
http://www.seomasterwordpress.com

Facebook Page
Be a fan of my Facebook page for more exclusive and Facebook-only SEO content:
http://www.facebook.com/pages/SEO-Master-WordPress/174532829318983

Blog
For more up-to-date SEO news you might want to read my blog:
http://www.seomasterwordpress.com/blog/

Twitter
Follow me on twitter for all-new professional SEO tips:
http://twitter.com/seomasterwp

Linkedin
Be a part of a growing SEO marketing community:
http://www.linkedin.com/pub/konstantinos-kreouzis/27/a26/539

Index

Symbols

A

B

C

D

E

F

www.ingramcontent.com/pod-product-compliance
Lightning Source LLC
LaVergne TN
LVHW071522070326
832902LV00002B/39